HARCOURT Math

Reteach Workbook

PUPIL EDITION
Grade 3

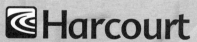
Orlando • Boston • Dallas • Chicago • San Diego
www.harcourtschool.com

California Edition

Copyright © by Harcourt, Inc.

All rights reserved. No part of this publication may be reproduced or transmitted in any form or by any means, electronic or mechanical, including photocopy, recording, or any information storage and retrieval system, without permission in writing from the publisher.

Permission is hereby granted to individual teachers using the corresponding student's textbook or kit as the major vehicle for regular classroom instruction to photocopy complete pages from this publication in classroom quantities for instructional use and not for resale.

Duplication of this work other than by individual classroom teachers under the conditions specified above requires a license. To order a license to duplicate this work in greater than classroom quantities, contact Customer Service, Harcourt, Inc., 6277 Sea Harbor Drive, Orlando, Florida 32887-6777. Telephone: 1-800-225-5425. Fax: 1-800-874-6418 or 407-352-3445.

HARCOURT and the Harcourt Logo are trademarks of Harcourt, Inc.

Printed in the United States of America

ISBN 0-15-320443-5

3 4 5 6 7 8 9 10   022   2004 2003

CONTENTS

Unit 1: UNDERSTAND NUMBERS AND OPERATIONS

Chapter 1: Place Value and Number Sense
1.1 Patterns on a Hundred Chart 1
1.2 Understand Place Value 2
1.3 Understand Numbers to 10,000 ... 3
1.4 Understand 10,000 4
1.5 Problem Solving Strategy: Use Logical Reasoning 5

Chapter 2: Compare, Order, and Round Numbers
2.1 Size of Numbers 6
2.2 Compare Numbers 7
2.3 Order Numbers 8
2.4 Problem Solving Skill: Identify Relationships 9
2.5 Round to Nearest 10 and 100 10
2.6 Round to Nearest 1,000 11

Chapter 3: Addition
3.1 Column Addition 12
3.2 Estimate Sums 13
3.3 Add 3-Digit Numbers 14
3.4 Add 3-Digit Numbers 15
3.5 Problem Solving Strategy: Predict and Test 16
3.6 Add Greater Numbers 17

Chapter 4: Subtraction
4.1 Estimate Differences 18
4.2 Subtract 3-Digit Numbers 19
4.3 Subtract 3-Digit Numbers 20
4.4 Subtract Greater Numbers 21
4.5 Problem Solving Skill: Estimate or Exact Answer 22
4.6 Algebra: Expressions and Number Sentences 23

Unit 2: MONEY AND TIME

Chapter 5: Use Money
5.1 Make Equivalent Sets 24
5.2 Problem Solving Strategy: Make a Table 25
5.3 Compare Amounts of Money 26
5.4 Make Change 27
5.5 Add and Subtract Money 28

Chapter 6: Understand Time
6.1 Time to the Minute 29
6.2 A.M. and P.M. 30
6.3 Elapsed Time 31
6.4 Use a Schedule 32
6.5 Use a Calendar 33
6.6 Problem Solving Skill: Sequence Events 34

Unit 3: MULTIPLICATION CONCEPTS AND FACTS

Chapter 7: Understand Multiplication
7.1 Algebra: Connect Addition and Multiplication 35
7.2 Multiply with 2 and 5 36
7.3 Arrays 37
7.4 Multiply with 3 38
7.5 Problem Solving Skill: Too Much/ Too Little Information 39

Chapter 8: Multiplication Facts Through 5
- 8.1 Multiply with 0 and 1 40
- 8.2 Multiply with 4 41
- 8.3 Problem Solving Strategy: Find a Pattern 42
- 8.4 Practice Multiplication 43
- 8.5 Algebra: Find Missing Factors 44

Chapter 9: Multiplication Facts and Strategies
- 9.1 Multiply with 6 45
- 9.2 Multiply with 7 46
- 9.3 Multiply with 8 47
- 9.4 Problem Solving Strategy: Draw a Picture 48
- 9.5 Algebra: Practice the Facts 49

Chapter 10: Multiplication Facts and Patterns
- 10.1 Multiply with 9 and 10 50
- 10.2 Algebra: Find a Rule 51
- 10.3 Algebra: Multiply with 3 Factors 52
- 10.4 Problem Solving Skill: Multistep Problems 53

Unit 4: DIVISION CONCEPTS AND FACTS

Chapter 11: Understand Division
- 11.1 The Meaning of Division 54
- 11.2 Relate Subtraction and Division ... 55
- 11.3 Algebra: Relate Multiplication and Division 56
- 11.4 Algebra: Fact Families 57
- 11.5 Problem Solving Strategy: Write a Number Sentence 58

Chapter 12: Division Facts Through 5
- 12.1 Divide by 2 and 5 59
- 12.2 Divide by 3 and 4 60
- 12.3 Divide with 0 and 1 61
- 12.4 Algebra: Write Expressions 62
- 12.5 Problem Solving Skill: Choose the Operation 63

Chapter 13: Division Facts Through 10
- 13.1 Divide by 6, 7, and 8 64
- 13.2 Divide by 9 and 10 65
- 13.3 Practice Division Facts Through 10 .. 66
- 13.4 Algebra: Find the Cost 67
- 13.5 Problem Solving Strategy: Work Backward 68

Unit 5: DATA, GRAPHING, AND PROBABILITY

Chapter 14: Collect and Record Data
- 14.1 Collect and Organize Data 69
- 14.2 Understand Data 70
- 14.3 Classify Data 71
- 14.4 Problem Solving Strategy: Make a Table 72

Chapter 15: Analyze and Graph Data
- 15.1 Problem Solving Strategy: Make a Graph 73
- 15.2 Read Bar Graphs 74
- 15.3 Make Bar Graphs 75
- 15.4 Line Plots 76
- 15.5 Locate Points on a Grid 77
- 15.6 Read Line Graphs 78

Chapter 16: Probability
- 16.1 Certain and Impossible 79
- 16.2 Likely and Unlikely 80
- 16.3 Possible Outcomes 81

16.4 Experiments 82
16.5 Predict Outcomes 83
16.6 Problem Solving Skill:
     Draw Conclusions 84

▶ Unit 6: MULTIPLY AND DIVIDE BY 1-DIGIT NUMBERS

▶ Chapter 17: Multiply by 1-Digit Numbers
17.1 Multiply 2-Digit Numbers 85
17.2 Record Multiplication 86
17.3 Practice Multiplication 87
17.4 Problem Solving Skill: Choose
     the Operation 88

▶ Chapter 18: Multiply Greater Numbers
18.1 Mental Math: Patterns in
     Multiplication 89
18.2 Problem Solving Strategy:
     Find a Pattern 90
18.3 Estimate Products 91
18.4 Multiply 3-Digit Numbers 92
18.5 Find Products Using Money 93
18.6 Practice Multiplication 94

▶ Chapter 19: Divide by 1-Digit Numbers
19.1 Divide with Remainders 95
19.2 Model Division of
     2-Digit Numbers 96
19.3 Record Division of
     2-Digit Numbers 97
19.4 Practice Division 98
19.5 Problem Solving Skill: Interpret
     the Remainder 99

▶ Chapter 20: Divide Greater Numbers
20.1 Mental Math: Patterns in
     Division 100
20.2 Estimate Quotients 101
20.3 Place the First Digit in
     the Quotient 102
20.4 Practice Division of
     3-Digit Numbers 103
20.5 Divide Amounts of Money 104
20.6 Problem Solving Strategy:
     Solve a Simpler Problem 105

▶ Unit 7: GEOMETRY

▶ Chapter 21: Solid and Plane Figures
21.1 Solid Figures 106
21.2 Combine Solid Figures 107
21.3 Line Segments and Angles 108
21.4 Types of Lines 109
21.5 Circles 110
21.6 Problem Solving Strategy:
     Break Problems into Simpler
     Parts 111

▶ Chapter 22: Polygons
22.1 Polygons 112
22.2 Congruence and Symmetry 113
22.3 Combine Plane Figures 114
22.4 Problem Solving Strategy:
     Find a Pattern 115

▶ Chapter 23: Triangles and Quadrilaterals
23.1 Triangles 116
23.2 Sort Triangles 117
23.3 Quadrilaterals 118
23.4 Sort Quadrilaterals 119
23.5 Problem Solving Skill: Identify
     Relationships 120

▶ Unit 8: MEASUREMENT

▶ Chapter 24: Customary Units
24.1 Length 121
24.2 Inch, Foot, Yard, and Mile 122

24.3 Capacity .... **123**.
24.4 Weight **124**
24.5 Ways to Change Units **125**
24.6 Algebra: Rules for
   Changing Units **126**
24.7 Problem Solving Skill: Use
   a Graph **127**

Chapter 25: Metric Units
25.1 Length **128**
25.2 Problem Solving Strategy: Make
   a Table **129**
25.3 Capacity: Liters and Milliliters ... **130**
25.4 Mass: Grams and Kilograms **131**
25.5 Measure Temperature **132**

Chapter 26: Perimeter, Area, and Volume
26.1 Perimeter **133**
26.2 Estimate and Find Perimeter **134**
26.3 Area of Plane Figures **135**
26.4 Area of Solid Figures **136**
26.5 Problem Solving Skill: Make
   Generalizations **137**
26.6 Estimate and Find Volume **138**

Unit 9: FRACTIONS AND DECIMALS

Chapter 27: Understand Fractions
27.1 Count Parts of a Whole **139**
27.2 Count Parts of a Group **140**
27.3 Equivalent Fractions **141**
27.4 Compare and Order Fractions ... **142**
27.5 Problem Solving Strategy: Make
   a Model **143**

Chapter 28: Add and Subtract Like Fractions
28.1 Add Fractions **144**
28.2 Add Fractions **145**
28.3 Subtract Fractions **146**
28.4 Subtract Fractions **147**
28.5 Problem Solving Skill:
   Reasonable Answers **148**

Chapter 29: Decimals and Fractions
29.1 Relate Fractions and Decimals .. **149**
29.2 Tenths **150**
29.3 Hundredths **151**
29.4 Read and Write Decimals **152**
29.5 Compare and Order Decimals ... **153**
29.6 Problem Solving Skill:
   Reasonable Answers **154**

Chapter 30: Decimals and Money
30.1 Relate Fractions and Money **155**
30.2 Relate Decimals and Money **156**
30.3 Add and Subtract Decimals
   and Money **157**
30.4 Problem Solving Strategy: Break
   Problems into Simpler Parts **158**

Name _____

LESSON 1.1

Patterns on a Hundred Chart

Numbers can be arranged in dot patterns.

Even numbers have pairs of dots.

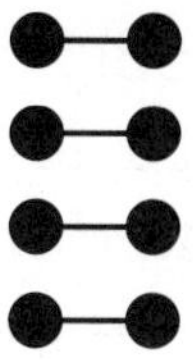

Odd numbers have pairs of dots, with one dot left over.

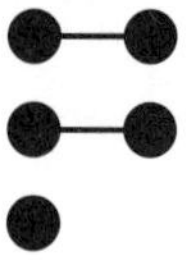

Write the number of dots in each set.
Circle the even numbers.

1. 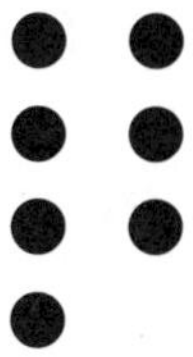   2.    3. 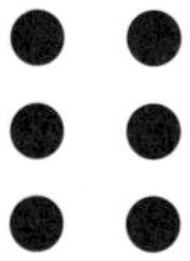   4.    5.    6.

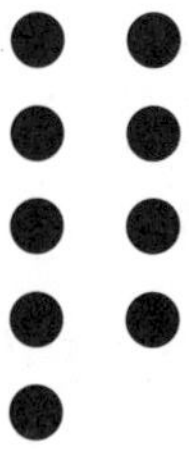

_____   _____   _____   _____   _____   _____

Even numbers end with 0, 2, 4, 6, or 8.

7. Circle the even numbers in the chart below.

1	2	3	4	5	6	7	8	9	10
11	12	13	14	15	16	17	18	19	20
21	22	23	24	25	26	27	28	29	30
31	32	33	34	35	36	37	38	39	40

Numbers that are not even are odd.

8. Odd numbers end with _____, _____, _____, _____, or _____.

Reteach   **RW1**

Name _____

LESSON 1.2

Understand Place Value

The symbols 0, 1, 2, 3, 4, 5, 6, 7, 8, and 9 are called **digits**.

Hundreds	Tens	Ones
5	2	6
500 +	20 +	6
= 526		

In the number 526 the value of the digit 5 is 5 hundreds, or 500. The value of the digit 2 is 2 tens, or 20. The value of the digit 6 is 6 ones, or 6. Read: "five hundred twenty-six"

Example 1
4̲78

The value of the digit 4 is 4 hundreds, or 400.
Say: "four hundred seventy-eight"

Example 2
1̲35

The value of the digit 3 is 3 tens, or 30.
Say: "one hundred thirty-five"

Example 3
62̲9

The value of the digit 9 is 9 ones, or 9.
Say: "six hundred twenty-nine"

Example 4
40̲1

A zero in the tens place shows that there are no tens.
Say: "four hundred one"

Write the value of the underlined digit.

1. 12̲5

   ones

2. 6̲58

   hundreds

3. 41̲6

   tens

4. 5̲48

   hundreds

5. 32̲4

   ones

6. 90̲6

   tens

7. 75̲6

   tens

8. 2̲30

   hundreds

9. 427̲

   ones

10. 64̲3

    tens

11. 580̲

    ones

12. 2̲09

    hundreds

RW2 Reteach

Name _____

LESSON 1.3

Understand Numbers to 10,000

Understanding large numbers is important for when you read or hear them.

A–C	D–F	G–H	I–J	K–L	M–N	O–Q	R–T	U–W	X–Z
Volume 1	Volume 2	Volume 3	Volume 4	Volume 5	Volume 6	Volume 7	Volume 8	Volume 9	Volume 10
1–100	101–200	201–300	301–400	401–500	501–600	601–700	701–800	801–900	901–1,000

Look at the books. If you were looking for page 564, in which volume would you look? You would look in Volume 6 because 564 falls between the numbers 501 and 600.

For 1–5, use the Table of Contents.

1. What subjects are in Chapter 4?

   Rocks, and minerals

Table of Contents	
Chapter 1	
Animals	pp. 3–126
Chapter 2	
Plants	pp. 127–201
Chapter 3	
Oceans	pp. 202–299
Chapter 4	
Rocks and Minerals	pp. 300–463

2. John wants to read about the Pacific Ocean. On which pages will he find the information?

   _202–299_

3. On which page does Chapter 2 begin?

   _127_

4. Eileen turns to page 157. What is she reading about?

   nothing

5. Frank opens the book to page 300. Which chapter did he open to?

   Chapter four

Reteach RW3

Name _____

LESSON 1.4

Understand 10,000

Ten Thousands	Thousands	Hundreds	Tens	Ones
2	3,	6	4	7

2 ten thousands	3 thousands	6 hundreds	4 tens	7 ones
20,000	3,000	600	40	7

20,000 + 3,000 + 600 + 40 + 7

You write it: 23,647.

You read it: "twenty-three thousand, six hundred forty-seven."

Write each number.

1. 60,000 + 4,000 + 500 + 90 + 4 _____

2. 40,000 + 8,000 + 400 + 70 + 5 _____

3. 20,000 + 300 + 50 + 2 _____

4. 10,000 + 3,000 + 400 + 40 _____

5. 50,000 + 9,000 + 20 + 4 _____

6. twenty-two thousand, five hundred forty-three

7. thirty-six thousand, two hundred twenty

8. fifty-five thousand, three hundred eighty-seven

9. ninety thousand, forty

10. eighty-three thousand, four hundred seven

11. eleven thousand, six hundred sixty-one

Name _____

LESSON 1.5

Problem Solving Strategy

Use Logical Reasoning

The Problem Bob said, "I am thinking of a 2-digit number. The sum of the digits is 12. Both digits are even. The tens digit is greater than the ones digit. What number am I thinking of?"

1	2	3	4	5	6	7	8	9	10
11	12	13	14	15	16	17	18	19	20
21	22	23	24	25	26	27	28	29	30
31	32	33	34	35	36	37	38	39	40
41	42	43	44	45	46	47	48	49	50
51	52	53	54	55	56	57	58	59	60
61	62	63	64	65	66	67	68	69	70
71	72	73	74	75	76	77	78	79	80
81	82	83	84	85	86	87	88	89	90
91	92	93	94	95	96	97	98	99	100

1. Underline what the problem asks.

2. What information will you use to answer the question?

   _____

   _____

Use logical reasoning to solve the problem.

3. Use the hundred chart. Find the 2-digit numbers having both even digits.

   _____

4. Use your answer to Problem 3. Find the numbers with the tens digit greater than the ones digit.

   _____

5. Use your answer to Problem 4. Find the number whose digits have a sum of 12. _____

6. So the number that Bob is thinking of is _____.

Use logical reasoning to solve the problem.

7. I am a number on the hundred chart. Both my digits are even. Both my digits are the same. The sum of my digits is 12. What number am I?

   _____

8. I am a number on the hundred chart. My ones digit is even. My tens digit is odd. My ones digit is 5 more than my tens digit. What numbers can I be?

   _____

Reteach   RW5

Name _____

LESSON 2.1

Size of Numbers

Benchmark numbers are useful numbers like 10, 25, 50, and 100 that help you see their relationship to other numbers.

You can use benchmark numbers to estimate the number of tiles on a floor.

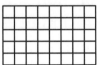

Choose a benchmark number, such as 10, and count that number of tiles.

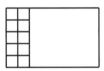

Estimate that there are about 4 groups of 10 tiles on the whole floor.
10 + 10 + 10 + 10 = 40

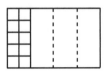

Estimate the number of tiles on each floor. Use the tiles that are shown as benchmarks.

1. 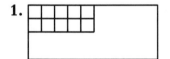   2. 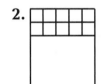   3.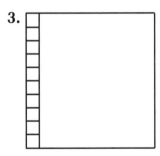

   _____   _____   _____

4. 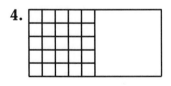   5. 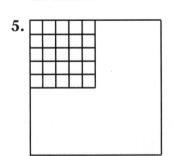   6.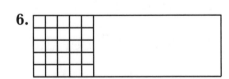

   _____   _____   _____

7. Are there more tiles on floor 1 or on floor 4?

   _____

RW6 Reteach

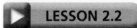

Name _____

Compare Numbers

Making models with base-ten blocks can help you compare numbers.

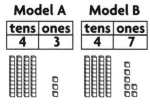

Step 1 Look at both models. Compare the place values, starting from the left.

Step 2 Look in the tens place. The models are the same, so continue to compare.

Step 3 Look in the ones place. The models are not the same.

Step 4 Model B shows more blocks in the ones place.

So, Model B shows the greater number.

Step 1 Look at both models. Compare the place values, starting from the left.

Step 2 Look in the hundreds place. The models are the same, so continue to compare.

Step 3 Look in the tens place. The models are not the same.

Step 4 Model B shows more blocks in the tens place.

So, Model B shows the greater number. (You don't need to look at the ones since the tens are different.)

Look at the models below. Write the greater number.

1.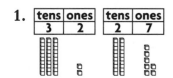

_____

2.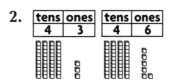

_____

3.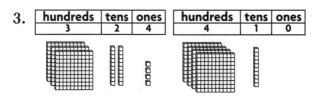

_____

4.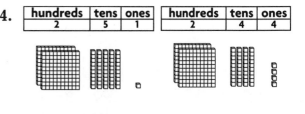

_____

Reteach **RW7**

Name _____

LESSON 2.3

Order Numbers

When you put more than two numbers in order, you compare the digits, starting with the place value farthest to the left. Set the numbers vertically to help you compare.

Put 351, 352, and 251 in order from least to greatest.

351 352 251

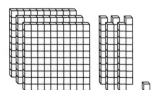 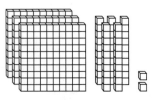 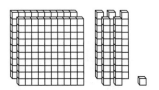

Step 1 Compare the hundreds of all three numbers.
3̲51
3̲52
2̲51
251 has the fewest hundreds, so it has the least value.

Step 2 Compare the tens of the other two numbers.
35̲1
35̲2
There is no difference, so look at the place value to the right.

Step 3 Now compare the ones.
351̲
352̲
1 < 2, so 351 < 352.

The numbers from least to greatest: 251, 351, 352

Write the numbers from least to greatest. Look at the numbers in the box to help you compare.

1. 65, 89, 64 | 65 89 64 | 2. 450, 458, 397 | 450 458 397 | 3. 263, 223, 323 | 263 223 323 |

_____ _____ _____

Write the numbers from greatest to least. Look at the numbers in the box to help you compare.

4. 265, 387, 254 | 265 387 254 | 5. 126, 654, 349 | 126 654 349 | 6. 458, 455, 465 | 458 455 465 |

_____ _____ _____

7. 23, 46, 15 | 23 46 15 | 8. 78, 84, 74 | 78 84 74 | 9. 112, 212, 115 | 112 212 115 |

_____ _____ _____

RW8 Reteach

Name _____

LESSON 2.4

Problem Solving Skill

Identify Relationships

UNDERSTAND your problem. You own a frozen yogurt store. You want to have a sale on flavors that sold less than 2,000 buckets last year. Which flavors should you have on sale?

FROZEN YOGURT SOLD	
Flavors	Buckets
Vanilla	3,000
Chocolate	2,600
Coffee	1,875
Strawberry	1,120
Fudge Swirl	651

PLAN Use a table to help solve your problem.

SOLVE The table shows how much frozen yogurt you sold last year. How are the numbers related? The numbers for buckets sold are in order from greatest to least. Coffee is the first flavor in the list that is less than 2,000. Since the numbers are listed from greatest to least, the flavors listed after coffee are all less than 2,000.

You should have a sale on coffee, strawberry, and fudge swirl yogurt.

For Problems 1–4, use the table.

Colored Golf Balls	
Red	3,956
Blue	2,608
Orange	1,473
Green	1,426
Yellow	850

1. Which color golf ball do people use the most?

   _____

2. Which color golf ball is used more, orange or blue?

   _____

3. Which two colors are picked about the same number of times?

4. Which color golf ball do people use the least

Reteach **RW9**

Round to Nearest 10 and 100

Rounding to the Nearest 10

How do you round numbers like 23 and 26 to the nearest ten?

- See what two tens a number is between. Both 23 and 26 are between 20 and 30.

- See which ten a number is closer to. If the ones digit is less than 5, round to the lesser ten. If the ones digit is 5 or greater, round to the greater ten.

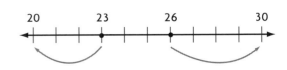

Rounding to the Nearest 100

How do you round numbers like 431 and 464 to the nearest hundred?

- See what two hundreds a number is between. Both 431 and 464 are between 400 and 500.

- See which hundred a number is closer to. If the tens digit is less than 5, round to the lesser hundred. If it is 5 or greater, round to the greater hundred.

Round to the nearest ten.

1. 46 2. 52 3. 35 4. 27

Round to the nearest hundred.

5. 134 6. 782 7. 893 8. 615

9. 125 10. 675 11. 832 12. 550

Name _____

LESSON 2.6

Round to Nearest 1,000

Rounding to the nearest thousand is just like rounding to the nearest ten and hundred.

The population of Cassandra's town is 6,643. Is the population about 6,000 or 7,000?

You are rounding to thousands, so look at the hundreds digit. Is it less than or greater than 5? Greater; so, you would round 6,643 to 7,000. The population is about 7,000.

Akira's town has a population of 5,237. How can you round that number to the nearest hundred?

You are rounding to hundreds, so look at the tens digit. Is it less than or greater than 5? Less; so, you would round 5,237 to 5,200. The population is about 5,200.

Round to the nearest hundred. Underline the digit that helps you know which way to round.

1. 369   2. 135   3. 2,187   4. 3,746

   _____   _____   _____   _____

5. 9,260   6. 1,742   7. 7,309   8. 5,691

   _____   _____   _____   _____

Round to the nearest thousand. Underline the digit that helps you know which way to round.

9. 6,809   10. 3,579   11. 2,469   12. 1,333

   _____   _____   _____   _____

13. 7,168 14. 5,702   15. 9,088   16. 4,625

   _____   _____   _____   _____

Reteach   RW11

Name _____

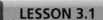
LESSON 3.1

Column Addition

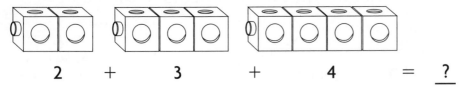

To find the sum of more than two addends, you can group the addends in different ways. The sum is always the same.

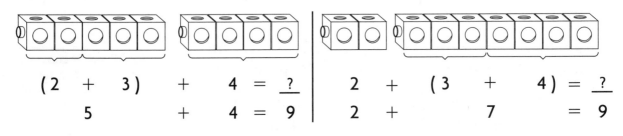

| (2 + 3) + 4 = ? | 2 + (3 + 4) = ? |
| 5 + 4 = 9 | 2 + 7 = 9 |

Add the numbers in ( ) first. Then find the sum.

1. (4 + 10) + 6 = _?_

   ___ + 6 = ___

   4 + (10 + 6) = _?_

   4 + ___ = ___

2. (3 + 2) + 18 = _?_

   ___ + 18 = ___

   3 + (2 + 18) = _?_

   3 + ___ = ___

3. (9 + 11) + 6 = _?_

   ___ + 6 = ___

   9 + (11 + 6) = _?_

   9 + ___ = ___

Group the addends by drawing ( ). Then find the sum.

4. 15 + 5 + 4 = ___
5. 3 + 12 + 6 = ___
6. 6 + 12 + 7 = ___
7. 13 + 4 + 2 = ___
8. 8 + 12 + 3 = ___
9. 16 + 6 + 6 = ___
10. 17 + 3 + 5 = ___
11. 22 + 8 + 2 = ___
12. 9 + 11 + 1 = ___

Find the sum.

13.   12
     13
  + 11

14.   23
     41
  + 10

15.   36
     14
  + 15

Name _____

LESSON 3.2

Estimate Sums

You can use a number line to help round to the nearest ten.

The numbers 61, 62, 63, and 64 are closer to 60 than 70.
Round **down** to 60.

The numbers 66, 67, 68, and 69 are closer to 70 than 60.
Round **up** to 70.

65 is exactly between 60 and 70.
Round 65 **up** to 70.

You can use rounding to estimate a sum. Round the numbers, then add.

```
    63  →    60
   +69      +70
Estimate    130
```

Round each number to the nearest ten and then estimate the sum. Use the number line.

1. 34 → ____
   +47 → + ____

   Estimate → ____

2. 39 → ____
   +45 → + ____

   Estimate → ____

Estimate the sum.

3. 312 → ____
   +588 → + ____

   Estimate → ____

4. 427 → ____
   +119 → + ____

   Estimate → ____

Reteach RW13

Add 3-Digit Numbers

Add 156 and 187.

Step 1

Add the ones. 6 + 7 = 13

Regroup 13 as 1 ten 3 ones.

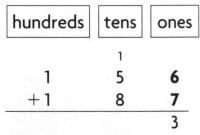

Circle ten ones when you can.

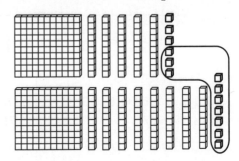

Step 2

Add the tens and the regrouped ten. 1 + 5 + 8 = 14

Regroup as 1 hundred and 4 tens.

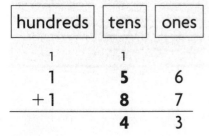

Circle ten tens when you can.

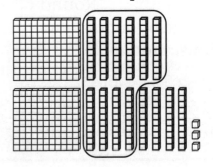

Step 3

Add the hundreds and the regrouped hundred. 1 + 1 + 1 = 3

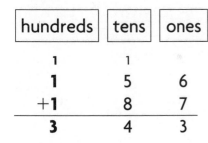

Use base-ten blocks to find each sum.

1. 3 7 6
   +2 4 8
   _____

2. 2 9 5
   +1 6 4
   _____

3. 7 1 7
   +2 6 9
   _____

4. 3 7 5
   +1 8 5
   _____

RW14 Reteach

Name _____

LESSON 3.4

Add 3-Digit Numbers

You can regroup: 10 ones as 1 ten

10 tens as 1 hundred

Add 248 + 395.

Step 1
Add the ones.
8 + 5 = 13 ones
13 ones =
1 ten 3 ones

Hundreds	Tens	Ones
	1	
2	4	8
+ 3	9	5
		3

Step 2
Add the tens.
1 + 4 + 9 = 14 tens
14 tens =
1 hundred 4 tens

Hundreds	Tens	Ones
1	1	
2	4	8
+ 3	9	5
	4	3

Step 3
Add the hundreds.
1 + 2 + 3 = 6 hundreds

Hundreds	Tens	Ones
1	1	
2	4	8
+ 3	9	5
6	4	3

Find the sum. Estimate to check.

1.
H	T	O
3	5	6
+1	2	8

2.
H	T	O
3	5	6
+4	9	1

3.
H	T	O
2	4	6
+6	7	8

4.
H	T	O
4	5	9
+3	5	3

5.
H	T	O
4	0	9
+4	5	9

6.
H	T	O
6	3	1
+2	8	7

7.
H	T	O
1	9	4
+1	8	9

8.
H	T	O
7	6	5
+1	6	5

Reteach

Name _____

LESSON 3.5

Problem Solving Strategy

Predict and Test

Sometimes you can find an answer by first predicting and then testing your answer.

Mary has 20 red and blue balloons at her party. She has 4 more red balloons than blue balloons. How many balloons of each color does she have?

	Blue	Red	Total	Notes
Prediction 1	5	5 + 4 = 9	5 + 9 = 14	too low
Prediction 2	10	10 + 4 = 14	10 + 14 = 24	too high
Prediction 3	8	8 + 4 = 12	8 + 12 = 20	just right

Mary has 8 blue balloons and 12 red balloons.

Use *predict and test* to solve. You may wish to make your own tables.

1. Peter delivers 110 newspapers on the weekend. He delivers 20 more newspapers on Sunday than on Saturday. How many newspapers does he deliver each day?

   _____

   _____

2. Paul is 5 years older than Lisa. The sum of their ages is 19. How old is each person?

   _____

3. Jesse has earned $40 more by washing cars than Tyrone has by raking leaves. Together they have $140. How much has each boy earned?

   _____

   _____

RW16 Reteach

Name _____

LESSON 3.6

Add Greater Numbers

Add 1,968 and 4,327.

Step 1

Estimate.

$$\begin{array}{r}1{,}968 \to 2{,}000\\+4{,}327 \to +4{,}000\\\hline 6{,}000\end{array}$$

Step 2

Add the ones. Regroup.
15 ones = 1 ten 5 ones

$$\begin{array}{r}{\scriptstyle 1}\\1{,}968\\+4{,}327\\\hline 5\end{array}$$

Step 3

Add the tens and the regrouped ten.

$$\begin{array}{r}{\scriptstyle 1}\\1{,}968\\+4{,}327\\\hline 95\end{array}$$

Step 4

Add the hundreds. Regroup.
12 hundreds = 1 thousand 2 hundreds

$$\begin{array}{r}{\scriptstyle 1\ \ 1}\\1{,}968\\+4{,}327\\\hline 295\end{array}$$

Step 5

Add the thousands and the regrouped thousand.

$$\begin{array}{r}{\scriptstyle 1\ \ 1}\\1{,}968\\+4{,}327\\\hline 6{,}295\end{array}$$

Step 6

Compare your answer to your estimate.

Since 6,000 is close to 6,295, the answer is reasonable.

Estimate. Then find the sum.

1. Estimate: _____

$$\begin{array}{r}3{,}758 \to \rule{1cm}{0.4pt}\\+2{,}169 \to +\rule{1cm}{0.4pt}\end{array}$$

2. Estimate: _____

$$\begin{array}{r}4{,}738 \to \rule{1cm}{0.4pt}\\+5{,}167 \to +\rule{1cm}{0.4pt}\end{array}$$

3. Estimate: _____

$$\begin{array}{r}1{,}426 \to \rule{1cm}{0.4pt}\\+5{,}939 \to +\rule{1cm}{0.4pt}\end{array}$$

4. Estimate: _____

$$\begin{array}{r}8{,}119 \to \rule{1cm}{0.4pt}\\+1{,}586 \to +\rule{1cm}{0.4pt}\end{array}$$

Reteach **RW17**

Name _____

LESSON 4.1

Estimate Differences

To estimate a difference, first round the numbers and then subtract.

Estimate the difference of 335 and 166.

Step 1
Round each number to the nearest hundred.

335 → 300
−166 → −200

Step 2
Subtract the rounded numbers.

300
− 200
─────
100

Example A
Estimate the difference of 4,613 and 1,399.
Round each number to the nearest thousand and then subtract.

4,613 → 5,000
− 1,399 → − 1,000
─────────
4,000

Example B
Estimate the difference of $10.75 and $5.82.
Round each number to the nearest dollar and then subtract.

$10.75 → $11
− $ 5.82 → −$ 6
─────────
$ 5

Estimate the difference by rounding.

1. 631 →
   − 258 → − _____

2. 82 →
   − 53 → − _____

3. $5.15 →
   −$2.64 → − _____

4. 6,671 →
   −1,257 → − _____

5. 4,001 →
   − 1,991 → − _____

6. 572 →
   − 289 → − _____

7. $10.28 →
   −$ 3.55 → − _____

8. 711 →
   − 468 → − _____

9. $7.95 →
   −$3.12 → − _____

RW18 Reteach

Name _____

▶ **LESSON 4.2**

Subtract 3-Digit Numbers

Subtract 135 from 324.

Step 1 Model 324 with base-ten blocks.

hundreds	tens	ones
3	2	4
−1	3	5

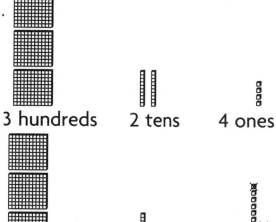

3 hundreds   2 tens   4 ones

Step 2 Regroup 2 tens
4 ones as 1 ten 14 ones.
Subtract the ones.

hundreds	tens	ones
	1	14
3	2̸	4̸
−1	3	5
		9

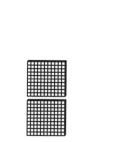

3 hundreds   1 ten   14 ones
                       − 5 ones
                         9 ones

Step 3 Regroup 3 hundreds
1 ten as 2 hundreds 11 tens.
Subtract the tens.

hundreds	tens	ones
2	11	14
3̸	2̸	4̸
−1	3	5
	8	9

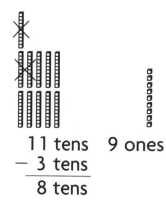

2 hundreds   11 tens   9 ones
             − 3 tens
               8 tens

Step 4 Subtract the hundreds.

hundreds	tens	ones
2	11	14
3̸	2̸	4̸
−1	3	5
1	8	9

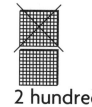

2 hundreds   8 tens   9 ones
− 1 hundred
  1 hundred

Use base-ten blocks to find each difference.

1. | H | T | O |
    |---|---|---|
    | 2 | 1 | 3 |
    | −1 | 4 | 8 |

2. | H | T | O |
    |---|---|---|
    | 4 | 3 | 5 |
    | −3 | 6 | 8 |

3. | H | T | O |
    |---|---|---|
    | 7 | 7 | 3 |
    | −5 | 6 | 5 |

4. | H | T | O |
    |---|---|---|
    | 3 | 4 | 6 |
    | −1 | 9 | 9 |

Reteach   RW19

LESSON 4.3

Name _____

Subtract 3-Digit Numbers

Sometimes you need to regroup more than once in a subtraction problem.

Subtract 546 − 379.

Step 1
Look at the ones.
9 > 6
Regroup.
4 tens 6 ones =
3 tens 16 ones

Subtract the ones.
16 − 9 = 7 ones

Hundreds	Tens	Ones
5	3̷4	1̷6̷6
− 3	7	9
		7

Step 2
Look at the tens.
7 > 3
Regroup.
5 hundreds 3 tens =
4 hundreds 13 tens

Subtract the tens.
13 − 7 = 6 tens

Hundreds	Tens	Ones
4̷5̷	1̷3̷4	1̷6̷6
− 3	7	9
	6	7

Step 3

Subtract the hundreds.
4 − 3 = 1 hundred

Hundreds	Tens	Ones
4̷5̷	1̷3̷4	1̷6̷6
− 3	7	9
1	6	7

Find the difference.

1. H T O
    8 2 9
    − 6 8 1

2. H T O
    4 3 5
    − 1 2 9

3. H T O
    5 2 4
    − 2 8 9

4. H T O
    8 2 5
    − 1 5 6

5. H T O
    3 5 6
    − 1 9 2

6. H T O
    4 3 5
    − 1 3 8

7. H T O
    3 9 4
    − 2 7 5

8. H T O
    7 7 6
    − 5 8 9

RW20 Reteach

Name _____ **LESSON 4.4**

Subtract Greater Numbers

3,000
−1,260
―――
?

How can you subtract 1,260 from 3,000?
You can't subtract from 0 tens or
0 hundreds, so regroup the thousands.

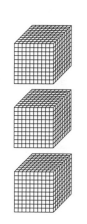 = 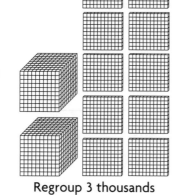 =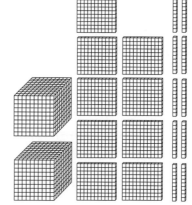

3 thousands

Regroup 3 thousands
as
2 thousands 10 hundreds

Regroup 2 thousands 10 hundreds
as
2 thousands 9 hundreds 10 tens

```
                  2 10              2  9
                                      10 10
  3,000           3̷,0̷00             3̷,0̷0̷0
 −1,260          −1,260            −1,2 6 0
 ―――――           ―――――             ―――――――
                                    1,7 4 0
```

Complete.

1. 5 thousands = 4 thousands ___ hundreds

   5 thousands = 4 thousands 9 hundreds ___ tens

2. 7 thousands = ___ thousands 10 hundreds

   7 thousands = 6 thousands ___ hundreds 10 tens

Show how you would regroup before subtracting.

3.
TH	H	T	O
6,	0	0	0
−2,	5	7	0

4.
TH	H	T	O
5,	0	0	0
−1,	5	1	1

5.
TH	H	T	O
8,	0	0	0
−4,	3	7	0

Reteach RW21

Name _____

LESSON 4.5

Problem Solving Skill

Estimate or Exact Answer

Estimate to find the answer when you do not need to know exactly how many or how much.

Give an exact answer when you want to be sure you do not have too many or too few of something.

Hal's Hobby Shop	
Item	Price
model	$6.89
glue	$1.89
paint	$1.09

Here are some examples.

Estimate to find the answer	Exact answer

Problem Morris has $12. Can he buy a model, glue, and paint? Estimate the total price of the items.
 	
model $6.89 → $7
glue $1.89 → $2
paint $1.09 → $1
                    $10
 	
Yes, Morris has enough money because $10 is less than $12.
	Problem Logan pays for paint that costs $1.09 with $2.00. How much change will she get? Find an exact number.
	
	   $2.00
	$-$ $1.09
	   $0.91
	
	Logan should get exactly $0.91 in change.

Write whether you need an exact answer or an estimate. Then solve.

1. Rene invited 16 girls, 12 boys, and 6 adults to help her wrap gifts for the residents of a nursing home. Which room should they meet in, Room #1 (15 seats), #2 (45 seats), or #3 (75 seats)?

2. Rene wants to be sure to have a pair of scissors for herself and each person that she has invited. How many scissors does she need?

RW22 Reteach

Name _____

LESSON 4.6

Algebra: Expressions and Number Sentences

Number sentences contain numbers, operations, and an equal sign.

Examples:
4 + 5 = 9   9 − 4 = 5

Some number sentences are *true*.

Examples:
3 + 5 = 8 True   9 − 7 = 2 True

Some number sentences are *false*.

Examples:
3 + 2 = 9 False   7 − 5 = 6 False

An **expression** is part of a number sentence. It contains numbers and operations. It does not contain an equal sign.

Examples
3 + 2   3 + 5   9 − 7
7 − 5   9 − 4   4 + 5

Write an expression for each.

1. Ron has 13 yellow apples and 25 red apples. How many apples does he have altogether?

   _____

2. Marsha bought 24 eggs. She used 8 for breakfast. How many eggs does she have now?

   _____

3. Kyle has 15 more pages to read than Linda. Linda has 12 pages to read. How many pages does Kyle have to read?

   _____

4. Jill bought 2 oranges, 3 apples, and 9 bananas. How many more bananas than oranges did she buy?

   _____

Write + or − to make the number sentence true.

5. 8 ◯ 4 = 12   6. 7 = 16 ◯ 9   7. 12 ◯ 3 = 9

8. 18 − 6 = 7 ◯ 5   9. 19 ◯ 3 = 22   10. 16 ◯ 11 = 27

11. 12 ◯ 7 = 3 + 2   12. 2 + 9 = 17 ◯ 6   13. 8 ◯ 8 = 16

Reteach   RW23

Name _____

LESSON 5.1

Make Equivalent Sets

Sets that are **equivalent** are worth the same amount.

The two sets of coins shown below are equivalent. Each set of coins has a value of $0.50.

Count: $0.25 $0.50	**Count:** $0.10 $0.20 $0.30 $0.40 $0.45 $0.50

Write the value of each set of coins, using a dollar sign and decimal point. Then draw a picture of an equivalent set.

1.

   _____

2.

   _____

3.

   _____

4.

   _____

RW24 Reteach

Name _____

LESSON 5.2

Problem Solving Strategy

Make a Table

Problem Gerald has three $1 bills, 4 quarters, 1 dime, 6 nickels, and 4 pennies. He buys a yo-yo for $3.28. How many different equivalent sets of bills and coins can he use to pay for the yo-yo?

1. Underline what the problem asks.

2. What information will you use?
   _____

3. Complete the table.

$1 bills	Quarters	Dimes	Nickels	Pennies	Value

4. Solve the problem. _____

5. How many different sets of coins can you use to show 14¢?

   _____

Dimes	Nickels	Pennies	Value

Reteach   RW25

Name _____

LESSON 5.3

Compare Amounts of Money

You can compare amounts of money by following these steps:

Step 1 Count each group of bills and coins.

Step 2 Write the total value of each group, using a dollar sign and decimal point.

Step 3 Compare the totals. Which amount is greater?

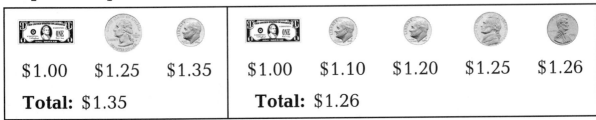

$1.00 $1.25 $1.35 $1.00 $1.10 $1.20 $1.25 $1.26

Total: $1.35   **Total:** $1.26

$1.35 is greater than $1.26.

Write the total value of each group of bills and coins, using a dollar sign and decimal point. Then circle the letter of the greater amount.

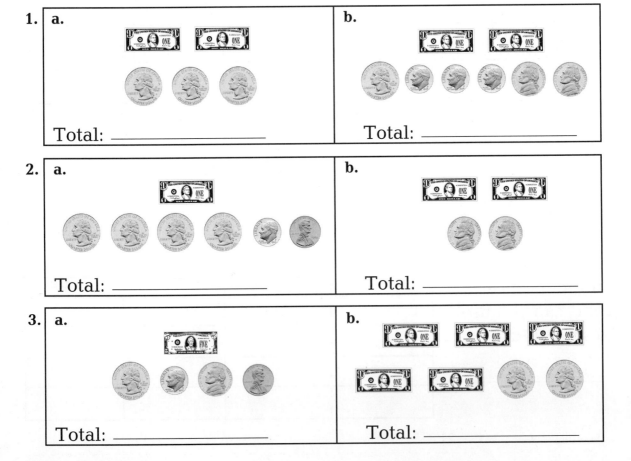

RW26 Reteach

Name _____   LESSON 5.4

Make Change

Mr. Cook sells a muffin that cost $0.79. Mrs. Lopez gives Mr. Cook a $1 bill. Mr. Cook counts out the change. He starts with the price of the muffin and begins counting on with coins that have the least value to make $1.00.

 $0.79 + + + =

$0.79 $0.80 $0.90 $1.00

money given: $1.00   change given: $0.21

Complete the table. Count the change. Draw the coin or bill that is missing in each set of change given.

	Money Given	Item Sold	Change Given
1.	$1.00	apple $0.35	nickel, dime, quarter ____ ____ ____ ____
2.	$1.00	ice cream $0.92	penny, penny, penny ____ ____ ____ ____ ____
3.	$1.00	shake $0.89	penny ____ ____
4.	$5.00	pizza $3.74	penny, quarter ____ ____ ____

Reteach RW27

Name _____

LESSON 5.5

Add and Subtract Money

Adding and subtracting money amounts is similar to adding and subtracting whole numbers.

Add. $\$2.15 + \$3.77 =$ ☐

Estimate the sum. Round to the nearest dollar.

$$\begin{array}{r}\$2.15 \rightarrow \$2.00 \\ +\$3.77 \rightarrow +\$4.00 \\ \hline \$6.00\end{array}$$

Step 1
Add money amounts as you would add whole numbers.
$$\begin{array}{r}\$2.15 \rightarrow \overset{1}{2}15 \\ +\$3.77 \rightarrow +377 \\ \hline 592\end{array}$$

Step 2
Write the sum in dollars and cents.
$$\begin{array}{r}\$2.15 \\ +\$3.77 \\ \hline \$5.92\end{array}$$

Compare the answer to the estimate. $5.92 is close to $6.00, so the answer is reasonable.

Subtract. $\$7.85 - \$5.53 =$ ☐

Estimate the difference. Round to the nearest dollar.

$$\begin{array}{r}\$7.85 \rightarrow \$8.00 \\ -\$5.53 \rightarrow -\$6.00 \\ \hline \$2.00\end{array}$$

Step 1
Subtract money amounts as you would subtract whole numbers.
$$\begin{array}{r}\$7.85 \rightarrow 785 \\ -\$5.53 \rightarrow -553 \\ \hline 232\end{array}$$

Step 2
Write the difference in dollars and cents.
$$\begin{array}{r}\$7.85 \\ -\$5.53 \\ \hline \$2.32\end{array}$$

$2.32 is close to $2.00, so the answer is reasonable.

Find the sum or difference. Estimate to check.

1. $\$2.34$
   $+\$1.49$

2. $\$5.83$
   $+\$3.49$

3. $\$9.62$
   $-\$2.17$

RW28 Reteach

Name _____

LESSON 6.1

Time to the Minute

How many minutes after 10:00 is it?

To count the number of minutes after the hour, follow these steps:

Start at the 12 on the clock. Count by fives as far as you can.

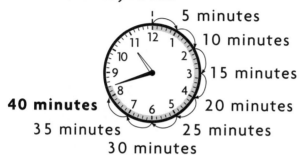

Then count by ones to where the minute hand is pointing. Add.

$40 + 2 = 42$

So, it is 42 minutes after 10, or 10:42.

Write how many fives and ones you count. Find the total number of minutes after the hour. Then write the time. The first one is done for you.

1.

    __15__ + __3__ = __18__

    The time is __10:18__.

2.

    ____ + ____ = ____

    The time is _____.

3.

    ____ + ____ = ____

    The time is _____.

4.

    ____ + ____ = ____

    The time is _____.

Reteach **RW29**

Name _____

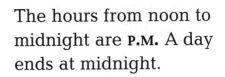

A.M. and P.M.

A day has 24 hours.

A new day starts just after midnight. The hours from midnight to noon are A.M.

The hours from noon to midnight are P.M. A day ends at midnight.

Marcie gets on the school bus at 8:05 A.M. The bus comes at five minutes after eight.

Kyle eats dinner with his family at 6:15 P.M. Dinner is ready at quarter past six.

Here is a diagram of one day.

Midnight	Sunrise	Noon	Sunset	Midnight
12:00	6:00	12:00	6:00	12:00
🌙	A.M.	☀	P.M.	🌙

Write the time, using A.M. or P.M.

1.
recess at school
_____

2.
eat breakfast
_____

3.
bedtime
_____

4.
sound asleep
_____

Write two ways you can read each time. Then write the time, using A.M. or P.M.

5.
Saturday morning basketball game

_____

_____

6.
a trip to the shoe store

_____

_____

RW30   Reteach

Name _____

LESSON 6.3

Elapsed Time

Elapsed time is the time that passes from the start of an activity to the end of that activity. To find the elapsed time, count the number of minutes between the start time and the end time.

Start: 6:15   End: 6:45   Elapsed time: 30 minutes

Remember:
- When the minute hand moves from one number to the next number on the clock, five minutes have passed.

Find the elapsed time.

	Start	End	Elapsed Time
1.	6:00	6:15	_____
2.	6:45	7:30	_____
3.	10:00	11:15	_____
4.	5:30	6:00	_____

Reteach RW31

Name _____

LESSON 6.4

Use a Schedule

A **schedule** is a table that lists activities or events and the times they happen.

You can use a schedule to find elapsed times of events. If you know the elapsed times, you can find start and end times on a schedule.

| THE ARTS CHANNEL SCHEDULE |||
Show	Time	Elapsed Time
Painting	9:00 A.M. — 10:30 A.M.	1 hour 30 minutes
Drawing	10:30 A.M. — 11:30 A.M.	▒
Pottery	11:30 A.M. — ▒	1 hour
Jewelry	▒ — 1:00 P.M.	30 minutes

For 1–4, use a clock with movable hands and the schedule above.

1. At what time does the painting show end?

   _____

2. How long is the drawing show?

   _____

3. At what time does the pottery show end?

   _____

4. At what time does the jewelry show begin?

   _____

RW32 Reteach

Name _____

LESSON 6.5

Use a Calendar

A **calendar** shows the days, weeks, and months of the year in order. Look at the calendars at the right.

Jack's cat had 4 kittens on May 15. It is now June 5. How many weeks old are the kittens?

Start at May 15. Count weeks by moving down the column of Wednesdays on the calendars until you reach June 5.

The kittens are 3 weeks old.

May 15, 2002
month day year

May 2002

Sun.	Mon.	Tue.	Wed.	Thu.	Fri.	Sat.
			1	2	3	4
5	6	7	8	9	10	11
12	13	14	(15)	16	17	18
19	20	21	22	23	24	25
26	27	28	29	30	31	

June 2002

Sun.	Mon.	Tue.	Wed.	Thu.	Fri.	Sat.
						1
2	3	4	(5)	6	7	8
9	10	11	12	13	14	15
16	17	18	19	20	21	22
23/30	24	25	26	27	28	29

For 1–4, use the calendars.

1. Two days before the kittens were born, Jack took his cat to the veterinarian. What date did he take his cat to the veterinarian?

   _____

2. The kittens first opened their eyes when they were 1 week and 1 day old. On what date did they first open their eyes?

   _____

3. Jack read that kittens are usually able to walk when they are 4 weeks old. On what date will Jack's kittens be 4 weeks old?

   _____

4. Jack needs to take his kittens to the veterinarian on June 26. How many weeks old will the kittens be on June 26?

   _____

Reteach RW33

Name _____

LESSON 6.6

Problem Solving Skill

Sequence Events

Bill is planning a pool party. Use the list of things to do to help him decide when these things should be done.

Complete. Use the calendar.

```
Today's Date: May 2
Party Date: May 25
Things to do:
• Send invitations in 5 days.
• Check weather 3 days before the party.
• Reserve pool 2 weeks before the party.
```

May 2002

Sun.	Mon.	Tue.	Wed.	Thu.	Fri.	Sat.
			1	②	3	4
5	6	7	8	9	10	11
12	13	14	15	16	17	18
19	20	21	22	23	24	㉕
26	27	28	29	30	31	

1. Find the date to send invitations. Start: May 2. Count on 5 days.

   _____

2. Find the date to check the weather. Start: May 25. Count back 3 days.

   _____

3. Find the date to reserve the pool. Start: May 25. Count back 2 weeks.

   _____

4. Write the things to do in order.

   Things to Do   Date

   _____

   _____

5. Use your answer to Problem 4. What will Bill do first?

   _____

6. Mr. Gordon's class planned trips to the zoo on May 28, to the space museum on May 16, and to the aquarium on May 23. Write the trips in order.

   _____

   _____

   _____

Name _____

 LESSON 7.1

Algebra: Connect Addition and Multiplication

Sasha and her 5 friends line up their tricycles. How many wheels are there?

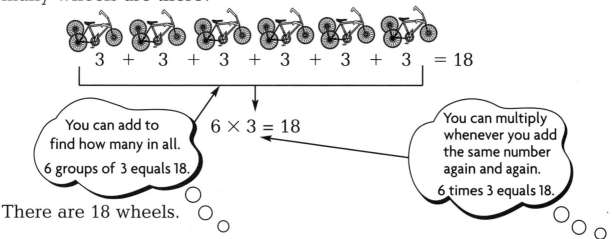

You can add to find how many in all.
6 groups of 3 equals 18.

$6 \times 3 = 18$

You can multiply whenever you add the same number again and again.
6 times 3 equals 18.

There are 18 wheels.

Complete.

1. How many buttons?

   ___ + ___ + ___ = ___

   ___ groups of ___ = ___

   ___ × ___ = ___

   There are ___ buttons.

2. How many eyes?

   ___ + ___ + ___ + ___ = ___

   ___ groups of ___ = ___

   ___ × ___ = ___

   There are ___ eyes.

3. How many crayons?

   ___ + ___ + ___ + ___ = ___

   ___ groups of ___ = ___

   ___ × ___ = ___

   There are ___ crayons.

4. How many dimes?

   ___ + ___ + ___ + ___ = ___

   ___ groups of ___ = ___

   ___ × ___ = ___

   There are ___ dimes.

Reteach RW35

Name _____

LESSON 7.2

Multiply with 2 and 5

Byron packs 5 pairs of socks.
How many socks in all does he pack?

He can solve the problem in 3 ways.

He can add.

2 + 2 + 2 + 2 + 2 = 10

He can skip-count.

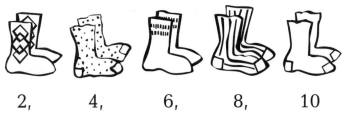

2,   4,   6,   8,   10

He can multiply.

$5 \times 2 = 10$

Solve each problem by adding, then by skip-counting, and then by multiplying.

1. 4 houses each have 5 windows. How many windows are there in all?

   _____
   _____
   _____

2. How many wings do 7 birds have?

   _____
   _____
   _____

3. If you have 3 nickels, how much money do you have?

   _____
   _____
   _____

Name _____

Arrays

An **array** shows objects in rows and columns.

You can use an array to help you **count** the total number in 2 rows of 4.

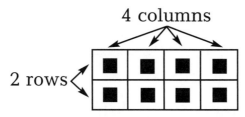

Count. There are a total of 8 tiles. So, 2 rows of 4 equals 8.

You can use an array to help you **multiply** the total number in 2 rows of 4.

Since 2 rows of 4 = 8, you know that 2 × 4 = 8.

Complete.

1.

    ___ rows of ___ = ___

2.

    ___ rows of ___ = ___

3.

    3 rows of 5 = ___

    3 × 5 = ___

4.

    5 rows of 3 = ___

    5 × 3 = ___

5.

    5 rows of 4 = ___

    5 × 4 = ___

6.

    4 rows of 5 = ___

    4 × 5 = ___

Name _____

LESSON 7.4

Multiply with 3

The Wings practiced 3 hours a day for 4 days. Use the number line to see how many hours they practiced in all.

The Hawks practiced 4 hours a day for 3 days. How many hours did they practice in all?

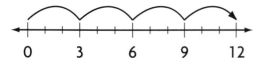

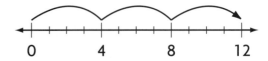

1. What multiplication sentence is shown on the number line?

   _____

2. What multiplication sentence is shown on the number line?

   _____

3. How many hours did the Wings practice in all?

   _____

4. How many hours did the Hawks practice in all?

   _____

5. Look at Exercises 1–4. They show the **Order Property of Multiplication**. They show that

   ____ × ____ and ____ × ____ both equal _____.

For 6–9, use the number line.

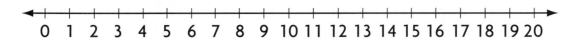

6. Mia drove 3 hours a day for 6 days. How many hours did she drive?

   _____

7. Ted drove 6 hours a day for 3 days. How many hours did he drive?

   _____

8. Fran earned $5 a week for 3 weeks. How much did she earn in all?

   _____

9. Graham earned $3 a week for 5 weeks. How much did he earn in all?

   _____

RW38 Reteach

Name _____

LESSON 7.5

Problem Solving Skill: Too Much/Too Little Information

Alexa and Carl are on the diving team. Alexa has been on the team 1 year longer than Carl. They practice diving with the team 2 hours three times a week.

How many hours a week do they practice diving with the team?	How many years has Alexa been on the team?
Ask Yourself What do I know? They practice ___ hours ___ times a week. Solve the problem. • Multiply. ___ × ___ = ___ hours	**Ask Yourself** What do I know? Alexa has been on the team ___ year longer than Carl. I need to know how many years Carl has been on the team. Can I find the information I need? No; the number of years Carl has been on the team is not given.

For 1–4, use the table. Write *a*, *b*, or *c* to tell whether the problem has:
a. too much information.
b. too little information.
c. the right amount of information.
Solve those with too much or the right amount of information.

Art Supplies	
box of colored pencils	$4
box of crayons	$2
pad of drawing paper	$5

1. Tyrone bought 2 boxes of crayons. He used a $10 bill to pay for them. How much change did Tyrone get?

   _____

2. Laura bought 3 items at the Art Supply store. She gave the clerk $20. How much change did she get?

   _____

3. Preston has $17. He bought 3 pads of drawing paper and 4 stencils. How much did he spend?

   _____

4. Rene bought 2 pads of drawing paper. Treva bought 3 boxes of colored pencils. How much did Treva spend?

   _____

Reteach RW39

Name _____

LESSON 8.1

Multiply with 0 and 1

- Pam put 1 muffin in each of 6 bags. How many muffins did she put in the bags?

You can draw a picture to find the answer.

Draw 6 bags, with 1 muffin in each bag.

1. What multiplication sentence can you write for

   6 bags with 1 muffin in each bag? _____

2. What happens when you multiply any number by 1?

   _____

- Pam gave each bag holding a muffin to a friend. Each friend ate the muffin. Now how many muffins are there?

You can draw another picture to find the answer.

Draw 6 empty bags, 0 muffins in each.

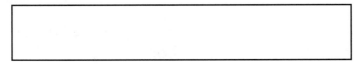

3. What multiplication sentence can you write for

   6 bags with 0 muffins in each bag? _____

4. What happens when you multiply any number by 0?

   _____

Find the product.

5. $1 \times 9 =$ _____   6. $0 \times 6 =$ _____   7. $8 \times 0 =$ _____   8. $5 \times 1 =$ _____

9. $7 \times 1 =$ _____   10. $0 \times 0 =$ _____   11. $3 \times 1 =$ _____   12. $9 \times 0 =$ _____

13. $1 \times 4 =$ _____   14. $0 \times 2 =$ _____   15. $6 \times 1 =$ _____   16. $5 \times 0 =$ _____

Name _____

LESSON 8.2

Multiply with 4

Nate counted his baseball cards. He made 9 stacks with 4 cards in each stack. How many cards did he have?

You can use a multiplication table to find the number of cards.

×	0	1	2	3	4	5	6	7	8	9
0	0	0	0	0	0	0	0	0	0	0
1	0	1	2	3	4	5	6	7	8	9
2	0	2	4	6	8	10	12	14	16	18
3	0	3	6	9	12	15	18	21	24	27
4	0	4	8	12	16	20	24	28	32	36
5	0	5	10	15	20	25	30	35	40	45
6	0	6	12	18	24	30	36	42	48	54
7	0	7	14	21	28	35	42	49	56	63
8	0	8	16	24	32	40	48	56	64	72
9	0	9	18	27	36	45	54	63	72	81

Step 1 Nate has 9 stacks of cards. So, 9 is a factor. Find the row marked 9.

Step 2 There are 4 cards in each stack. So, 4 is a factor. Find the column marked 4.

Step 3 Find the box where row 9 and column 4 meet. This box shows the product of 9 and 4.

Using the multiplication table, you find that Nate had 36 cards.

Name the factors in each of the problems below. Then, use the multiplication table to solve.

1. Mia uses 7 ribbons on every card she makes. Mia wants to make 4 cards. How many ribbons does she need?

   Factors: _____

   _____

2. Akio gets an allowance of $4 each week. He spends $3 and saves the rest. How much does he save every 8 weeks?

   Factors: _____

   _____

3. Norman practices basketball 1 hour on school days and 2 hours each day of the weekend. How many hours does he practice in 4 weeks?

   Factors: _____

   _____

4. Tamisha counted the dimes in her bank. She made 6 stacks with 4 dimes in each stack. How many dimes did she count?

   Factors: _____

   _____

Reteach

Name _____

LESSON 8.3

Problem Solving Strategy
Find a Pattern

The Problem The houses on Bill's street follow a pattern. The first seven houses on his street are numbered 1, 5, 8, 12, 15, 19, 22. What is the rule for the pattern? What are the next three house numbers?

1. Underline what the problem asks.
2. What information will you use to answer the question?

   _____

3. Is there information you will not use? If so, what?

   _____

4. What strategy can you use to solve the problem?

   _____

5. Use a number line to find the pattern. Then write the rule.

   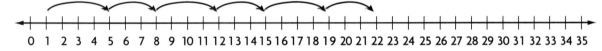

   _____

6. What are the next three numbers? _____

Use *find a pattern* to solve.

7. Tammy's pattern is 1, 3, 7, 9, 13, and 15. What is the rule? What are the next four numbers in her pattern?

8. Bryant's pattern is 1, 6, 11, 16, 21, and 26. What is the rule? What are the next four numbers in his pattern?

9. Melinda's pattern is 20, 40, 60, 80, and 100. What is the rule? What are the next four numbers in her pattern?

10. Edward's pattern is 4, 6, 5, 7, 6, 8, and 7. What is the rule? What are the next four numbers in his pattern?

RW42 Reteach

Practice Multiplication

There are many ways to find a product. Here are a few of them.

Find 2 × 5.

Example A	Example B
You can make equal groups.  So, 2 × 5 = 10.	You can make an array.  So, 2 × 5 = 10.
Example C You can skip count on a number line. 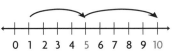 So, 2 × 5 = 10.	**Example D** You can use a fact you already know. Think: 5 + 5 = 10 So, 2 × 5 = 10.
Example E You can use a multiplication table. Think: The product is found where row 2 and column 5 meet. So, 2 × 5 = 10.	

Find the product.

1. 7 × 3 = _____
2. 5 × 4 = _____
3. 2 × 8 = _____
4. 6 × 2 = _____
5. 8 × 5 = _____
6. 3 × 9 = _____
7. 0 × 5 = _____
8. 4 × 9 = _____
9. 3 × 8 = _____
10. 2 × 7 = _____
11. 8 × 4 = _____
12. 7 × 4 = _____

Name _____ LESSON 8.5

Algebra: Find Missing Factors

When you know the product and one factor, you can use skip-counting to find the missing factor.

Find each missing factor.

Example A	Example B
___?___ × 4 = 28 ↑ ↑ ↑ missing factor factor product Skip-count by 4s until you reach 28. 4, 8, 12, 16, 20, 24, 28 You counted 7 numbers. So, **7** × 4 = 28.	6 × ___?___ = 30 ↑ ↑ ↑ factor missing factor product Skip-count by 6s until you reach 30. 6, 12, 18, 24, 30 You counted 5 numbers. So, 6 × **5** = 30.

Find the missing factor. You may wish to skip-count or use a multiplication table.

1. ____ × 3 = 12   2. 8 × ____ = 40   3. ____ × 2 = 14

4. 9 × ____ = 27   5. ____ × 4 = 8   6. 2 × ____ = 16

7. ____ × 7 = 7   8. ____ × 5 = 45   9. 9 × ____ = 18

10. 5 × ____ = 30   11. ____ × 9 = 36   12. ____ × 4 = 28

13. ____ × 5 = 40   14. 5 × ____ = 25   15. 6 × ____ = 18

16. 3 × ____ = 6   17. 4 × ____ = 36   18. ____ × 4 = 20

19. 4 × ____ = 24   20. ____ × 9 = 9   21. 3 × ____ = 24

RW44   Reteach

Name _____

LESSON 9.1

Multiply with 6

An **array** shows objects in rows and columns.
An array can be used to show a multiplication sentence.

Show 3 × 6.

The array has 3 rows.
Each row has 6 circles.
3 × 6 = 18

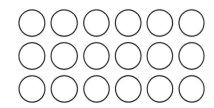

You can break apart an array
to help you find a product.

Add the products of the two
smaller arrays.

9 + 9 = 18

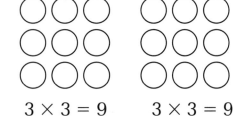

3 × 3 = 9   3 × 3 = 9

Complete the number sentence to show how many in all.

1. ○○○○○○
   ○○○○○○

   2 × 6 = _____

2. ○○○○○○
   ○○○○○○
   ○○○○○○
   ○○○○○○

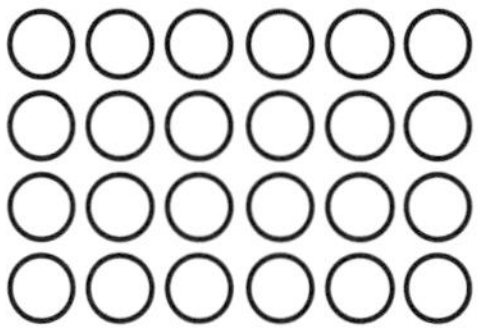

   4 × 6 = _____

3. ○○○○○○
   ○○○○○○
   ○○○○○○
   ○○○○○○
   ○○○○○○

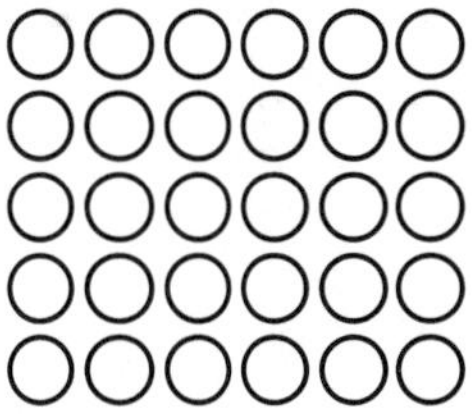

   5 × 6 = _____

Draw the array for each exercise below.
Write the product.

4. 6 rows of 2

6 × 2 = _____

5. 1 row of 6

1 × 6 = _____

6. 6 rows of 4

6 × 4 = _____

Reteach **RW45**

Name _____

LESSON 9.2

Multiply with 7

You can multiply two numbers in either order.
The product is the same.

Find 3 × 7.

   7 × 1 = 7
7 × 2 = 14
7 × 3 = 21

3 rows of 7
3 × 7 = 21

Find 7 × 3.

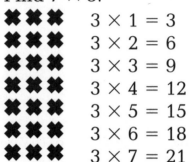   3 × 1 = 3
3 × 2 = 6
3 × 3 = 9
3 × 4 = 12
3 × 5 = 15
3 × 6 = 18
3 × 7 = 21

7 rows of 3
7 × 3 = 21

Complete the number sentences.

1.

2 × 7 = _____

7 × 2 = _____

2.

4 × 7 = _____

7 × 4 = _____

Find the product for each pair of factors.

3. 7   1
   ×1 ×7

4. 7   8
   ×8 ×7

5. 7   6
   ×6 ×7

6. 7   5
   ×5 ×7

7. 7   9
   ×9 ×7

8. 7   0
   ×0 ×7

9. 7   3
   ×3 ×7

10. 7   4
   ×4 ×7

RW46 Reteach

Name _____

LESSON 9.3

Multiply with 8

You can use the multiplication facts you know to learn new facts. The examples show two different ways to learn 6 × 8.

$$
\begin{array}{r} 5 \times 8 \\ + 1 \times 8 \\ \hline 6 \times 8 \end{array}
\quad
\begin{array}{r} 40 \\ + 8 \\ \hline 48 \end{array}
\qquad
\begin{array}{r} 3 \times 8 \\ + 3 \times 8 \\ \hline 6 \times 8 \end{array}
\quad
\begin{array}{r} 24 \\ + 24 \\ \hline 48 \end{array}
$$

Complete the number sentences.

1. 3 × 8 = _____
   1 × 8 = _____
   4 × 8 = _____

2. 2 × 8 = _____
   2 × 8 = _____
   4 × 8 = _____

Find the product. You may use the facts that are given to help you.

3. 5 × 8 = 40
   1 × 8 = 8
   6 × 8 = _____

4. 4 × 8 = 32
   1 × 8 = 8
   5 × 8 = _____

5. 3 × 8 = 24
   3 × 8 = 24
   6 × 8 = _____

6. 7 × 8 = 56
   2 × 8 = 16
   9 × 8 = _____

Find the product for each pair of factors.

7. 8   7
   ×7   ×8

8. 8   5
   ×5   ×8

9. 8   9
   ×9   ×8

10. 8   3
   ×3   ×8

11. 4   8
   ×8   ×4

12. 0   8
   ×8   ×0

13. 6   8
   ×8   ×6

14. 2   8
   ×8   ×2

Reteach RW47

Name _____

LESSON 9.4

Problem Solving Strategy
Draw a Picture

The Problem   Carlotta glued 2 rows of 8 buttons on a paper to show an array for 16. What is another way she could have arranged the buttons in equal rows?

1. Underline what the problem asks.
2. Circle the information you will use to answer the question.
3. What strategy can you use to solve the problem?

   _____

4. Draw a picture of the buttons Carlotta glued on a paper.

5. Draw a picture of a new array, using the same buttons. What array did you draw?

   _____

Use *draw a picture* to solve.

6. Lance has a total of 12 buttons. How could he arrange the buttons so that he has equal rows?

7. Fay makes 6 rows with 4 buttons in each row. What is another way she could arrange the buttons in equal rows?

8. Lucy has a total of 9 buttons. How can she arrange the buttons so that her array is the same number of buttons wide as it is long?

9. Spencer had 15 buttons. He made 3 rows of buttons. How many buttons were in each row?

RW48   Reteach

Name _____

LESSON 9.5

Algebra: Practice the Facts

Here are some ways you have learned to find 5 × 8.

A. Break an array into known facts.

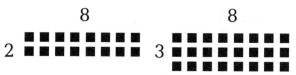

$2 \times 8 = 16 \qquad 3 \times 8 = 24$

$16 + 24 = 40$

$5 \times 8 = 40$

B. Use a multiplication table.

×	0	1	2	3	4	5	6	7	8
0	0	0	0	0	0	0	0	0	0
1	0	1	2	3	4	5	6	7	8
2	0	2	4	6	8	10	12	14	16
3	0	3	6	9	12	15	18	21	24
4	0	4	8	12	16	20	24	28	32
5	0	5	10	15	20	25	30	35	40
6	0	6	12	18	24	30	36	42	48
7	0	7	14	21	28	35	42	49	56
8	0	8	16	24	32	40	48	56	64

$5 \times 8 = 40$

C. Use doubles.

To find an 8's fact, you can double a 4's fact.

Think: $5 \times 4 = 20$

Double the product.
$20 + 20 = 40$

$5 \times 8 = 40$

D. Use the Order Property of Multiplication.

Try switching the order of the factors:

Think: $8 \times 5 = 40$, so $5 \times 8 = 40$.

$5 \times 8 = 40$

Find each product.

1. $7 \times 8 =$ _____
2. $5 \times 9 =$ _____
3. $8 \times 8 =$ _____

4. $6 \times 9 =$ _____
5. $8 \times 9 =$ _____
6. $4 \times 9 =$ _____

7. $0 \times 7 =$ _____
8. $7 \times 6 =$ _____
9. $9 \times 6 =$ _____

10. $2 \times 9 =$ _____
11. $8 \times 4 =$ _____
12. $6 \times 4 =$ _____

13. $1 \times 9 =$ _____
14. $7 \times 7 =$ _____
15. $6 \times 6 =$ _____

16. $4 \times 8 =$ _____
17. $3 \times 9 =$ _____
18. $7 \times 9 =$ _____

19. $8 \times 0 =$ _____
20. $2 \times 7 =$ _____
21. $6 \times 8 =$ _____

Reteach **RW49**

Name _____

LESSON 10.1

Multiply with 9 and 10

You can use facts of 10 to find facts of 9.

$8 \times 9 = \underline{\ ?\ }$

First think of the facts of 10.	Then find 8×9.
Skip-count by tens 9 times. 10, 20, 30, 40, 50, 60, 70, 80, 90 So, $1 \times 10 = 10$ $5 \times 10 = 50$ $2 \times 10 = 20$ $6 \times 10 = 60$ $3 \times 10 = 30$ $7 \times 10 = 70$ $4 \times 10 = 40$ $8 \times 10 = 80$ $9 \times 10 = 90$	The 10's fact that can help me is $8 \times 10 = 80$ Next, subtract the first factor, 8. $80 - 8 = 72$ Since $80 - 8 = 72$, $8 \times 9 = 72$.

You can use patterns to find facts of 9.

- The tens digit is one less than the number being multiplied by 9.

  $8 \times 9 = \underline{\ 72\ }$

- The sum of the digits in the product is **9**. $7 + 2 = 9$

Find the product.

1. $7 \times 10 =$ _____ $70 - 7 =$ _____ $7 \times 9 =$ _____	2. $9 \times 10 =$ _____ $90 - 9 =$ _____ $9 \times 9 =$ _____	3. $6 \times 10 =$ _____ $60 - 6 =$ _____ $6 \times 9 =$ _____

4. $3 \times 9 =$ _____   5. $5 \times 10 =$ _____   6. $9 \times 8 =$ _____

7. $0 \times 9 =$ _____   8. $1 \times 10 =$ _____   9. $9 \times 5 =$ _____

10. $2 \times 9 =$ _____   11. $9 \times 7 =$ _____   12. $4 \times 10 =$ _____

13. $1 \times 9 =$ _____   14. $10 \times 3 =$ _____   15. $9 \times 3 =$ _____

RW50   Reteach

Name _____

LESSON 10.2

Algebra: Find a Rule

Each person in Bob's computer lab has 10 fingers. There are 8 people in his computer lab. How many fingers is this?

Think: **1** person has 10 fingers.
2 people have 20 fingers
3 people have 30 fingers

Organize your work in a table. Look for a pattern. Write a rule.

People	1	2	3	4	5	6	7	8
Fingers	10	20	30	40	50	60	70	?

Pattern
The number of fingers equals the number of people times 10.

Rule
Multiply the number of people by 10.

Since $8 \times 10 = 80$, then there are 80 fingers in the computer lab.

Write a rule for each table. Then complete the table.

1.
Chairs	1	2	3	4	5	6
Legs	4	8	12	16		

Rule: _____

2.
Dollars	4	5	6	7	8	9
Dimes	40	50	60			

Rule: _____

3.
Toys	1	2	3	4	5	6
Rings	2	4	6	8		

Rule: _____

4.
Quarters	4	5	6	7	8
Nickels	20	25	30		

Rule: _____

5.
Couches	1	2	3	4	5
Cushions	4	8	12		

Rule: _____

6.
Quizzes	5	6	7	8	9
Answers	30	36	42		

Rule: _____

Reteach RW51

Name _____

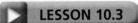 LESSON 10.3

Algebra: Multiply with 3 Factors

The **Grouping Property of Multiplication** states that when the grouping of factors is changed, the product remains the same.

$$3 \times 2 \times 5 = \underline{\ ?\ }$$

Multiply the first two factors first.	Multiply the numbers in ( ) first.	Multiply the last two factors first.
$(3 \times 2) \times 5 = \underline{\ ?\ }$ ↓ $6 \times 5 = 30$		$3 \times (2 \times 5) = \underline{\ ?\ }$ ↓ $3 \times 10 = 30$

Find each product.

1. $(7 \times 1) \times 3 = \underline{\ ?\ }$
   ↓
   ____ $\times 3 =$ ____

2. $8 \times (5 \times 2) = \underline{\ ?\ }$
   ↓
   $8 \times$ ____ $=$ ____

3. $(3 \times 3) \times 6 = \underline{\ ?\ }$
   ↓
   ____ $\times 6 =$ ____

4. $(1 \times 3) \times 9 =$ ____

5. $(2 \times 4) \times 5 =$ ____

6. $4 \times (2 \times 2) =$ ____

7. $9 \times (0 \times 9) =$ ____

8. $(1 \times 5) \times 10 =$ ____

9. $(3 \times 9) \times 0 =$ ____

10. $2 \times (3 \times 3) =$ ____

11. $4 \times (4 \times 2) =$ ____

12. $7 \times (2 \times 3) =$ ____

13. $8 \times (2 \times 1) =$ ____

14. $(5 \times 2) \times 9 =$ ____

15. $(1 \times 8) \times 4 =$ ____

16. $4 \times (2 \times 3) =$ ____

17. $(3 \times 2) \times 2 =$ ____

18. $6 \times (2 \times 3) =$ ____

19. $(8 \times 1) \times 8 =$ ____

20. $10 \times (3 \times 2) =$ ____

21. $(0 \times 7) \times 10 =$ ____

22. $6 \times (4 \times 2) =$ ____

23. $(3 \times 3) \times 3 =$ ____

24. $2 \times (2 \times 2) =$ ____

25. $(1 \times 1) \times 1 =$ ____

26. $4 \times (2 \times 4) =$ ____

27. $(2 \times 4) \times 9 =$ ____

Name _____

LESSON 10.4

Problem Solving Skill: Multistep Problems

A multistep problem is a problem which uses more than one step in order to solve it.

To earn money for a vacation, Bryan walked 3 dogs. Rene walked 4 dogs. They got paid $2 for each dog they walked. How much money did they earn in all?

Step 1 Find how much money Bryan earned.	__3__ × __$2__ = __$6__ Bryan earned __$6__.
Step 2 Find how much money Rene earned.	__4__ × __$2__ = __$8__ Rene earned __$8__.
Step 3 Find how much money they earned in all.	__$6__ + __$8__ = __$14__ So, they earned $14 in all.

Solve.

1. Paul read 315 pages in 3 days. He read 109 the first day and 105 the second day. How many pages did he read the third day?

   Step 1 How much did Paul read altogether on the first and second days? _____

   Step 2 How many pages did he read the third day?

   _____

2. Rita bought 4 cartons of eggs. Each carton had 8 eggs. Her family ate 10 of the eggs. How many eggs were left?

   Step 1 How many eggs did Rita buy? _____

   Step 2 How many eggs were left? _____

3. Robbie earns $2 for each car she washes. She earns $6 for each car she waxes. Robbie washed 4 cars and waxed 3 cars. How much did she earn? _____

4. Nancy drove 400 miles in three days. She drove 113 on each of the first two days. How many miles did she drive on the third day?

   _____

Reteach RW53

Name _____

LESSON 11.1

The Meaning of Division

Use division when you want to separate objects into groups of equal size.

You have 12 marbles.

You want to make 3 groups of equal size.

You put 4 marbles in each group.

Say: 12 divided by 3 equals 4.
Write: 12 ÷ 3 = 4

Solve.

1.

   How many in all? _____

   How many groups? _____

   How many in each group? _____

   12 ÷ 2 = _____

2.

   How many in all? _____

   How many groups? _____

   How many in each group? _____

   12 ÷ 6 = _____

3.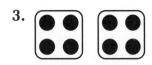

   How many in all? _____

   How many groups? _____

   How many in each group? _____

   8 ÷ 2 = _____

4.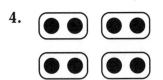

   How many in all? _____

   How many groups? _____

   How many in each group? _____

   8 ÷ 4 = _____

RW54 Reteach

Name _____

LESSON 11.2

Relate Subtraction and Division

Division is like repeated subtraction.

How many groups of 2 are there in 8?

Start at 8 on the number line.
Count back 2 spaces at a time until you reach 0.

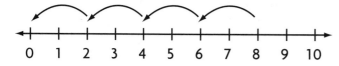

$$\begin{array}{r}8\\-2\\\hline 6\end{array} \quad \begin{array}{r}6\\-2\\\hline 4\end{array} \quad \begin{array}{r}4\\-2\\\hline 2\end{array} \quad \begin{array}{r}2\\-2\\\hline 0\end{array}$$

You can subtract 2 from 8 four times because there are 4 groups of 2 in 8.

So, $8 \div 2 = 4$.

Find the quotient. You may use the number line to help.

1. $12 \div 2 =$ _____

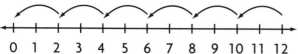

2. $12 \div 6 =$ _____

3. $12 \div 3 =$ _____

0 1 2 3 4 5 6 7 8 9 10 11 12

4. $12 \div 4 =$ _____

0 1 2 3 4 5 6 7 8 9 10 11 12

5. $10 \div 2 =$ _____

0 1 2 3 4 5 6 7 8 9 10

6. $10 \div 5 =$ _____

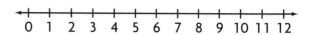

0 1 2 3 4 5 6 7 8 9 10

7. $9 \div 3 =$ _____

0 1 2 3 4 5 6 7 8 9 10

8. $8 \div 4 =$ _____

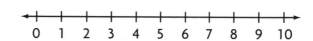

0 1 2 3 4 5 6 7 8 9 10

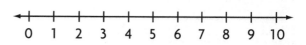

Reteach   RW55

Name _____

Algebra: Relate Multiplication and Division

Multiplication and division are opposite or **inverse operations**.

$$3 \times 5 = 15$$
factor factor product

3 groups of 5 equal 15 in all.

$$15 \div 3 = 5$$
dividend divisor quotient

15 divided into 3 equal groups equals 5.

Write the missing number for each number sentence.

1.

    4 × ____ = 12

    12 ÷ 4 = ____

2.

    3 × ____ = 12

    12 ÷ 3 = ____

3.

    6 × ____ = 18

    18 ÷ 6 = ____

4.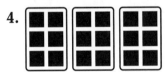

    3 × ____ = 18

    18 ÷ 3 = ____

Complete.

5. 4 × ____ = 20, so 20 ÷ 4 = ____

6. 4 × ____ = 16, so 16 ÷ 4 = ____

7. 3 × ____ = 15, so 15 ÷ 3 = ____

8. 5 × ____ = 30, so 30 ÷ 5 = ____

9. 2 × ____ = 16, so 16 ÷ 2 = ____

10. 7 × ____ = 21, so 21 ÷ 7 = ____

11. 3 × ____ = 9, so 9 ÷ 3 = ____

12. 5 × ____ = 35, so 35 ÷ 5 = ____

RW56 Reteach

Name _____

LESSON 11.4

Algebra: Fact Families

Use multiplication and division to tell about the cookies in opposite ways.

Use multiplication to put same-size groups together.

$3 \times 4 = 12$
or
$4 \times 3 = 12$

Use division to separate the total into same-size groups.

$12 \div 3 = 4$
or
$12 \div 4 = 3$

The four number sentences are called a **fact family**. Each of the four sentences uses the same numbers.

Complete each fact family.

1. 

   $4 \times 2 = 8$
   _____
   _____
   _____

2.

   $3 \times 2 = 6$
   _____
   _____
   _____

3.

   $3 \times 5 = 15$
   _____
   _____
   _____

4.

   $6 \times 3 = 18$
   _____
   _____
   _____

5.

   $6 \times 4 = 24$
   _____
   _____
   _____

6.

   $7 \times 3 = 21$
   _____
   _____
   _____

Reteach **RW 57**

Name _____

LESSON 11.5

Problem Solving Strategy

Write a Number Sentence

You can write a number sentence to help you solve a problem.

Example: There are 18 students in Josh's class. They are working in groups of 3. How many groups are there in all?

$$\underset{\substack{\uparrow \\ \text{number of} \\ \text{students}}}{18} \div \underset{\substack{\uparrow \\ \text{number} \\ \text{in each group}}}{3} = \underset{\substack{\uparrow \\ \text{number of} \\ \text{groups}}}{6}$$

Remember

Multiply
- when you are joining groups of equal size.
- when you know the size of the groups and the number of same-size groups.

Divide
- when you are separating a total into groups of equal size.
- when you know the total.
- when you know either the number of same-size groups or the number in each group.

Write a number sentence to solve. Then write the answer.

1. Mary rode her bicycle 4 miles every day for 5 days. How many miles did she ride in all?

2. Twelve campers want to canoe. Each canoe holds 3 people. How many canoes are needed?

3. Jeff earns $3 an hour for raking leaves. How many hours does he need to work to earn $15?

4. Jackie made a cartoon book that is 8 pages long. There are 4 cartoons on each page. How many cartoons are in the book?

RW58   Reteach

Name _____

LESSON 12.1

Divide by 2 and 5

You can use the multiplication facts you know to find quotients.

Here are two examples.

Example A	Example B
16 ÷ 2 = ? ↑ ↑ ↑ dividend divisor quotient Think: 2 × ? = 16 2 × **8** = 16 So, 16 ÷ 2 = 8 or 2)$\overline{16}$ with 8 on top	30 ÷ 5 = ? ↑ ↑ ↑ dividend divisor quotient Think: 5 × ? = 30 5 × **6** = 30 So, 30 ÷ 5 = 6 or 5)$\overline{30}$ with 6 on top

Find each quotient.

1. 18 ÷ 2 = _____   2. 35 ÷ 5 = _____   3. 10 ÷ 2 = _____

   Think: 2 × ___ = 18   Think: 5 × ___ = 35   Think: 2 × ___ = 10

4. 50 ÷ 5 = _____   5. 14 ÷ 2 = _____   6. 6 ÷ 2 = _____

   Think: 5 × ___ = 50   Think: 2 × ___ = 14   Think: 2 × ___ = 6

7. 40 ÷ 5 = _____   8. 2 ÷ 2 = _____   9. 20 ÷ 5 = _____

10. 20 ÷ 2 = _____   11. 25 ÷ 5 = _____   12. 45 ÷ 5 = _____

13. 8 ÷ 2 = _____   14. 12 ÷ 2 = _____   15. 5 ÷ 5 = _____

16. 5)$\overline{20}$ 17. 2)$\overline{18}$ 18. 5)$\overline{30}$ 19. 5)$\overline{50}$

20. 2)$\overline{10}$ 21. 2)$\overline{12}$ 22. 5)$\overline{35}$ 23. 5)$\overline{40}$

Reteach RW59

Name _____

LESSON 12.2

Divide by 3 and 4

You can use the multiplication facts you know to find quotients.

Here are two examples.

Example A	Example B
15 ÷ 3 = _?_ ↑ ↑ ↑ dividend divisor quotient Think: 3 × _?_ = 15 3 × **5** = 15 So, 15 ÷ 3 = 5 or 3)15̄ with 5 on top	28 ÷ 4 = _?_ ↑ ↑ ↑ dividend divisor quotient Think: 4 × _?_ = 28 4 × **7** = 28 So, 28 ÷ 4 = 7 or 4)28̄ with 7 on top

Find each quotient.

1. 18 ÷ 3 = _____
   Think: 3 × ___ = 18

2. 32 ÷ 4 = _____
   Think: 4 × ___ = 32

3. 12 ÷ 4 = _____
   Think: 4 × ___ = 12

4. 40 ÷ 4 = _____
   Think: 4 × ___ = 40

5. 16 ÷ 4 = _____
   Think: 4 × ___ = 16

6. 6 ÷ 3 = _____
   Think: 3 × ___ = 6

7. 21 ÷ 3 = _____

8. 20 ÷ 4 = _____

9. 24 ÷ 3 = _____

10. 24 ÷ 4 = _____

11. 27 ÷ 3 = _____

12. 30 ÷ 3 = _____

13. 8 ÷ 4 = _____

14. 12 ÷ 3 = _____

15. 3 ÷ 3 = _____

16. 3)21̄

17. 4)32̄

18. 3)9̄

19. 4)20̄

20. 4)28̄

21. 3)27̄

22. 4)36̄

23. 4)4̄

RW60   Reteach

Name _____

LESSON 12.3

Divide with 0 and 1

$6 \div 6 = ?$ Divide 6 counters into 6 groups. There is 1 in each group. $6 \div 6 = 1$	$6 \div 1 = ?$ Divide 6 counters into 1 group.  There are 6 in each group. $6 \div 1 = 6$	$0 \div 6 = ?$ Divide 0 counters into 6 groups.  There are 0 in each group. $0 \div 6 = 0$
Any number divided by itself is 1.	Any number divided by 1 is that number.	Zero divided by any number is 0.

Find each quotient.

1. $8 \div 8 =$ _____
2. $4 \div 1 =$ _____
3. $0 \div 5 =$ _____
4. $7 \div 1 =$ _____
5. $3 \div 3 =$ _____
6. $9 \div 9 =$ _____
7. $0 \div 3 =$ _____
8. $1 \div 1 =$ _____
9. $0 \div 7 =$ _____
10. $8 \div 1 =$ _____
11. $2 \div 2 =$ _____
12. $4 \div 4 =$ _____
13. $7 \div 7 =$ _____
14. $5 \div 1 =$ _____
15. $0 \div 2 =$ _____

Look at Exercises 1–15 again. If a number is divided by itself, put a triangle around the quotient. If a number is divided by 1, put a circle around the quotient. If the dividend is 0, put a box around the quotient.

Find each missing factor.

16. $1 \times$ _____ $= 8$
17. $7 \times$ _____ $= 0$
18. $1 \times$ _____ $= 5$
19. _____ $\times 8 = 0$
20. $4 \times$ _____ $= 4$
21. _____ $\times 1 = 3$
22. _____ $\times 3 = 3$
23. _____ $\times 3 = 0$
24. $6 \times$ _____ $= 6$

Reteach RW61

Name _____

LESSON 12.4

Algebra: Write Expressions

An expression is part of a number sentence. You can use the operation symbols (+, −, ×, ÷) in expressions to show how to solve problems.

To choose an operation symbol for an expression, think about how the action is taking place.

Multiply	**Add**
• Combine equal groups.	• Combine groups.
Six friends each ate 4 crackers. How many crackers did the friends eat altogether?	The friends ate 3 crackers the first hour. They ate 7 crackers the second hour. How many crackers did they eat in all?
the expression: 6 × 4	**the expression:** 3 + 7
Divide	**Subtract**
• Share equally. • Make equal groups.	• Take away. • Compare. • Separate.
Three friends shared 15 crackers equally. How many crackers did each friend get?	Bill ate 3 fewer crackers than Jane. Jane ate 5 crackers. How many crackers did Bill eat?
the expression: 15 ÷ 3	**the expression:** 5 − 3

Write an expression to describe each problem.

1. Five friends each made 8 greeting cards. How many greeting cards did the friends make altogether?

   _____

2. Mel made 9 greeting cards. He sent 6 of them. How many greeting cards does he have left?

   _____

3. Erin made 4 greeting cards. Louise made 5 greeting cards. How many greeting cards did they make altogether?

   _____

4. Sarah bought stamps for her greeting cards. The stamps came in 5 equal rows. Sarah bought 30 stamps. How many stamps were in each row?

   _____

Reteach

Name _____

LESSON 12.5

Problem Solving Skill:
Choose the Operation

The table below shows examples of problems in which you add, subtract, multiply, or divide.

There are 18 children and 6 adults at the park. How many people are at the park?	**Add** - You are joining groups of different size. 18 + 6 = 24 24 people
There are 10 boys and 8 girls at the park. How many more boys are there than girls?	**Subtract** - You are comparing two different amounts. 10 − 8 = 2 2 more boys
There are 3 sets of swings. Each swing set has 4 swings. How many swings are there in all?	**Multiply** - You are joining groups of equal size. 3 × 4 = 12 12 swings
The 18 students in a class divide into teams of 6 to play a game. How many teams of students are there?	**Divide** - You are separating a total into groups of equal size. 18 ÷ 6 = 3 3 teams

---

Choose the operation you need to use. Write *add*, *subtract*, *multiply*, or *divide*. Then solve.

1. Mrs. Shaw buys 6 packages of muffins. There are 4 muffins in each package. How many muffins does she buy?

   _____

2. Louisa bakes 12 small cookies and 9 large cookies. How many cookies does she bake in all?

   _____

3. Mr. Mason uses 20 apples to make pies. He uses 5 apples in each pie. How many pies does he make?

   _____

4. A large pizza costs $9.00, and a small pizza costs $5.25. How much more does the large pizza cost than the small one?

   _____

Reteach **RW63**

Name _____

LESSON 13.1

Divide by 6, 7, and 8

You can use the multiplication facts you know to find quotients.

Here are three examples.

Example A	Example B	Example C
$24 \div 6 = \underline{\ ?\ }$ ↑ ↑ ↑ dividend divisor quotient Think: $6 \times \underline{\ ?\ } = 24$ $6 \times 4 = 24$ So, $24 \div 6 = 4$ or $6\overline{)24}$.	$28 \div 7 = \underline{\ ?\ }$ ↑ ↑ ↑ dividend divisor quotient Think: $7 \times \underline{\ ?\ } = 28$ $7 \times 4 = 28$ So, $28 \div 7 = 4$ or $7\overline{)28}$.	$48 \div 8 = \underline{\ ?\ }$ ↑ ↑ ↑ dividend divisor quotient Think: $8 \times \underline{\ ?\ } = 48$ $8 \times 6 = 48$ So, $48 \div 8 = 6$ or $8\overline{)48}$.

Complete.

1. $18 \div 6 = \underline{\ \ \ }$
   Think: $6 \times \underline{\ \ \ } = 18$

2. $32 \div 8 = \underline{\ \ \ }$
   Think: $8 \times \underline{\ \ \ } = 32$

3. $14 \div 7 = \underline{\ \ \ }$
   Think: $7 \times \underline{\ \ \ } = 14$

4. $72 \div 8 = \underline{\ \ \ }$
   Think: $8 \times \underline{\ \ \ } = 72$

5. $42 \div 6 = \underline{\ \ \ }$
   Think: $6 \times \underline{\ \ \ } = 42$

6. $49 \div 7 = \underline{\ \ \ }$
   Think: $7 \times \underline{\ \ \ } = 49$

7. $6 \div 6 = \underline{\ \ \ }$

8. $21 \div 7 = \underline{\ \ \ }$

9. $24 \div 8 = \underline{\ \ \ }$

10. $40 \div 8 = \underline{\ \ \ }$

11. $36 \div 6 = \underline{\ \ \ }$

12. $56 \div 7 = \underline{\ \ \ }$

13. $64 \div 8 = \underline{\ \ \ }$

14. $12 \div 6 = \underline{\ \ \ }$

15. $30 \div 6 = \underline{\ \ \ }$

16. $6\overline{)54}$

17. $7\overline{)63}$

18. $7\overline{)42}$

19. $6\overline{)48}$

20. $8\overline{)56}$

21. $8\overline{)16}$

22. $7\overline{)0}$

23. $6\overline{)54}$

RW64 Reteach

Name _____

LESSON 13.2

Divide by 9 and 10

You can use the multiplication facts you know to find quotients.

Here are two examples.

Example A	Example B
$72 \div 9 = \underline{}$ ↑ dividend ↑ divisor ↑ quotient Think: $9 \times \underline{} = 72$ $9 \times \mathbf{8} = 72$ So, $72 \div 9 = 8$ or $9\overline{)72}$ with quotient 8	$30 \div 10 = \underline{}$ ↑ dividend ↑ divisor ↑ quotient Think: $10 \times \underline{} = 30$ $10 \times \mathbf{3} = 30$ So, $30 \div 10 = 3$ or $10\overline{)30}$ with quotient 3

Complete.

1. $18 \div 9 =$ _____
   Think: $9 \times$ ___ $= 18$

2. $20 \div 10 =$ _____
   Think: $10 \times$ ___ $= 20$

3. $36 \div 9 =$ _____
   Think: $9 \times$ ___ $= 36$

4. $50 \div 10 =$ _____
   Think: $10 \times$ ___ $= 50$

5. $45 \div 9 =$ _____
   Think: $9 \times$ ___ $= 45$

6. $80 \div 10 =$ _____
   Think: $10 \times$ ___ $= 80$

7. $90 \div 10 =$ _____

8. $10 \div 10 =$ _____

9. $54 \div 9 =$ _____

10. $27 \div 9 =$ _____

11. $63 \div 9 =$ _____

12. $70 \div 10 =$ _____

13. $40 \div 10 =$ _____

14. $81 \div 9 =$ _____

15. $60 \div 10 =$ _____

16. $9\overline{)36}$

17. $10\overline{)80}$

18. $9\overline{)9}$

19. $9\overline{)72}$

20. $10\overline{)60}$

21. $9\overline{)63}$

22. $10\overline{)100}$

23. $9\overline{)90}$

Reteach RW65

Name _____

LESSON 13.3

Practice Division Facts Through 10

One way to recall a division fact is to think of a related multiplication fact.

Find 18 ÷ 3.

Think: How many groups of 3 are in 18?
or What number multiplied times 3 equals 18?

? × 3 = 18

6 × 3 = 18, so 18 ÷ 3 = **6**.

Complete.

1. ___ × 4 = 24, so 24 ÷ 4 = ___
2. ___ × 10 = 30, so 30 ÷ 10 = ___
3. ___ × 5 = 35, so 35 ÷ 5 = ___
4. ___ × 6 = 36, so 36 ÷ 6 = ___
5. ___ × 8 = 80, so 80 ÷ 8 = ___
6. ___ × 7 = 21, so 21 ÷ 7 = ___

Find the quotient. Think about multiplication facts that have 5 as a factor.

7. 25 ÷ 5 = ___
8. 40 ÷ 5 = ___
9. 15 ÷ 5 = ___
10. 10 ÷ 5 = ___
11. 45 ÷ 5 = ___
12. 20 ÷ 5 = ___
13. 35 ÷ 5 = ___
14. 5 ÷ 5 = ___
15. 30 ÷ 5 = ___

Find the quotient. Think about multiplication facts that have 9 as a factor.

16. 63 ÷ 9 = ___
17. 72 ÷ 9 = ___
18. 18 ÷ 9 = ___
19. 45 ÷ 9 = ___
20. 27 ÷ 9 = ___
21. 54 ÷ 9 = ___
22. 9 ÷ 9 = ___
23. 36 ÷ 9 = ___
24. 81 ÷ 9 = ___

RW66 Reteach

Name _____

LESSON 13.4

Algebra: Find the Cost

You can multiply to find the cost of multiple items.

Example A

Alex bought 5 sandwiches. Each sandwich cost $3. How much did Alex spend?

5 × $3 = $15
↑ ↑ ↑
number of   cost of   total
sandwiches   one   spent

Alex spent a total of $15 on sandwiches.

You can divide to find the cost of one item.

Example B

Silva paid $24 for 8 sandwiches. How much does one sandwich cost?

$24 ÷ 8 = $3
↑ ↑ ↑
total   number of   cost
spent   sandwiches   of one

One sandwich costs $3.

For 1–9, one notebook costs $3 and one highlighter costs $2.
Find the cost of each number of items.

1. 2 highlighters

   ___ × ___ = ___

2. 3 notebooks

   ___ × ___ = ___

3. 4 highlighters

   ___ × ___ = ___

4. 9 notebooks

   ___ × ___ = ___

5. 7 highlighters

   ___ × ___ = ___

6. 6 notebooks

   ___ × ___ = ___

7. 5 highlighters

   ___

8. 8 notebooks

   ___

9. 5 notebooks

   ___

For 10–18, find the cost of one of each item.

10. 8 hats cost $72

    ___ ÷ ___ = ___

11. 6 stamps cost $12

    ___ ÷ ___ = ___

12. 4 T-shirts cost $40

    ___ ÷ ___ = ___

13. 5 toy trucks cost $25

    ___ ÷ ___ = ___

14. 3 books cost $27

    ___ ÷ ___ = ___

15. 9 CD's cost $81

    ___ ÷ ___ = ___

16. 3 pies cost $30

    ___

17. 7 belts cost $49

    ___

18. 10 watches cost $80

    ___

Reteach **RW67**

Name _____

Problem Solving Strategy

Work Backward

Tiko spent 4 days building a 98 cm bridge out of craft sticks. He built 24 cm of the bridge on Tuesday, 29 cm of the bridge on Wednesday, and 27 cm on Thursday. How much of the bridge did Tiko build on Monday?

UNDERSTAND

1. What are you asked to do? _____

2. What information will you use? _____

PLAN

3. What strategy can you use to solve the problem?

_____

SOLVE

4. How can you work backward to solve the problem?

_____

5. How much of the bridge did he build on Monday? _____

CHECK

6. Look back. Does your answer make sense? _____

RW68 Reteach

Name _____

LESSON 14.1

Collect and Organize Data

Information about people or things is called **data.** Data can be collected and organized in different ways.

Tally Table

A **tally table** uses tally marks to record data. Each tally shows the kind of pants one person is wearing.

Kinds of Pants	
Pants	Tally
Dark	///
Striped	ḦḦ /
Light	//

Frequency Table

A **frequency table** uses numbers to record data. This table shows the number of tallies used in the tally table.

Kinds of Pants	
Pants	Number
Dark	3
Striped	6
Light	2

Remember, tally marks are grouped by fives.

Complete the tally table and the frequency table for the picture below.

1.

Kinds of Shirts	
Shirt	Tally
Stripes	
Polka-dots	
Flowers	
Logos	
Plain	

2.

Kinds of Shirts	
Shirt	Number
Stripes	
Polka-dots	
Flowers	
Logos	
Plain	

Reteach RW69

Name _____

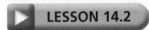

Understand Data

This is a survey question.

What is your favorite flavor of ice cream?
   Chocolate
   Vanilla
   Strawberry

The survey question about ice cream was asked of 14 people. Their answers are the results of the survey.

Look at the tally table at the right. The results of the survey are recorded using tally marks. It's an easy way to see what flavor of ice cream people like best.

Chocolate

Vanilla

Strawberry

OUR FAVORITE ICE-CREAM FLAVORS	
Flavor	Tally
Chocolate	‖‖‖‖ |||
Vanilla	||||
Strawberry	||

For 1, use the survey results in the tally table below.

1. List the drinks in order from the most to the least chosen.

   _____

   _____

   _____

OUR FAVORITE DRINKS	
Drink	Tally
Kooky-Kola	|||
Strawberry Surprise	||
Rooting Root Beer	‖‖‖‖ |||
Paradise Punch	‖‖‖‖

For 2–3, use the frequency table.

2. How many people were surveyed?

   _____

3. How many more people answered yes than no?

   _____

DO YOU OWN A PET?	
Answer	Number
Yes	32
No	27

Name _____

▶ **LESSON 14.3**

Classify Data

You can group, or classify, data in many different ways. Look at the fish at the right.

Fish can be grouped by size, color, shape, number of fins, the pattern on their bodies, and so on.

The chart at the right has the fish grouped by size and pattern.

FISH			
	Dots and Stripes	Stripes	Dots
Large	1	2	1
Small	2	4	1

For 1–6, use the table above.

1. How many of the fish have dots only?

2. How many large fish are there?

3. How many small fish have stripes only?

4. How many small fish are there?

5. How many of the fish have stripes only?

6. How many fish are there in all?

7. In Rebecca's class there are 12 girls and 15 boys. Of the girls, 8 have blue backpacks, 3 have red backpacks, and the rest have black backpacks. Of the boys, 2 have blue backpacks, 4 have red backpacks, and the rest have black backpacks. Make a frequency table to group the students in the class.

Reteach **RW71**

Problem Solving Strategy

Make a Table

Sam and Matilda are doing an experiment with two spinners. They will spin each pointer 20 times to find the sum they spin the most often and the least often. After spinning each of the two pointers, they will add the two numbers they spun. They will need to record the sums. What would be the best way to organize and record what happens in their experiment?

Step 1 Make a table. List all of the different possible sums.

Step 2 Spin the pointers 20 times each. Record one tally mark for each sum.

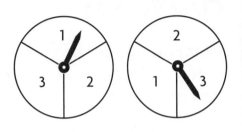

SPINNER EXPERIMENT	
Sum	Number of Spins
2							
3				
4				
5						
6				

Make a table to solve.

1. Joe and Maria are doing an experiment with two spinners. They will spin the pointers on the spinners and then record the results. They will spin the pointers 50 times. Show how they can organize a table about their experiment.

   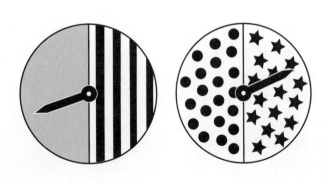

2. Heather is doing an experiment with two spinners. One spinner has two sections: a light section and a dark section. The other spinner has two sections: A and B. In the experiment she will spin the pointer and record the result 50 times. Show how she can organize a table about her experiment.

   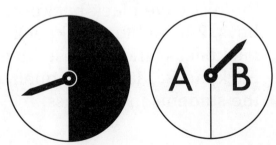

Name _____

LESSON 15.1

Problem Solving Strategy

Make a Graph

A pictograph uses pictures to show information. Use the data from this frequency table to make a pictograph.

- Title the pictograph *Favorite Pets*.
- Label column 1 *Kind of Pet*.
- Label column 2 *Number of Students*.
- List the kinds of pets in the first column.
- Make a key that shows that each picture equals 2 students.
- Draw pictures to show the number of students for each row.

FAVORITE PETS	
Kind of Pet	Number of Students
Dog	16
Cat	10

Key: Each ___ = _____ students.

Find Dog on the frequency table. Locate the number next to the name. The key says each symbol equals 2 students. Since 16 ÷ 2 = 8, draw 8 pictures.

To complete the pictograph, follow the same steps for Cat.

Make a pictograph that shows the data from the frequency table below. The key should show that each picture stands for 5 students.

FAVORITE DR. SEUSS® STORY	
Story	Number of Votes
Green Eggs and Ham	25
Hop on Pop	15
The Foot Book	20

Reteach RW73

Name _____

Read Bar Graphs

A **bar graph** uses bars to show data. In a **vertical** bar graph, the bars go up. In a **horizontal** bar graph, the bars go across from left to right.

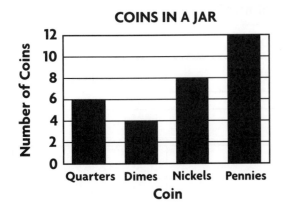
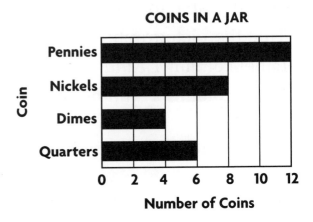

Reading a Vertical Bar Graph
- The title is on top.
- Each bar stands for something.
- Run your finger to the top of a bar.
- Read the number to the left of the top of the bar to see how many.
- The numbers of the **scale** on the left show the amounts of the items.

Reading a Horizontal Bar Graph
- The title is on top.
- Each bar stands for something.
- Run your finger to the far right of a bar.
- Read the number below the end of the bar to see how many.
- The numbers of the **scale** on the bottom show the amounts of the items.

For 1–4, use the bar graphs above.

1. Find the number of nickels in the jar. _____

2. Which coin is there the most of? the fewest of? How can you tell?
_____
_____

3. Find the number of pennies in the jar. _____

4. How many more pennies are there than quarters? _____

RW74 Reteach

Name _____

Make Bar Graphs

Make a horizontal bar graph of the data in the frequency table.

- Use the same title.
- Label each row with the names of the meals.
- Use a scale of 2. Write the numbers along the bottom of the graph
- Write *Number of Votes* under the scale. Write *Meal* beside the names of the meals.
- For each meal, make a bar as long as the number of votes.

| OUR FAVORITE MEAL ||
Meal	Number of Votes
Breakfast	6
Snack	4
Lunch	10
Dinner	2

Breakfast

0

For 1–3, use the completed bar graph.

1. For which meal is the bar the longest? _____

2. For which meal is the bar the shortest? _____

3. If the number of votes for Snack had been 5, where would the bar end?

_____

Reteach **RW75**

Name _____

LESSON 15.4

Line Plots

Ms. Ryan is teaching a cartooning class for students ages 8 to 12. She made a line plot. This **line plot** shows the number of students of each age in the class.
How many students are 10 years old?

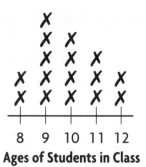

Ages of Students in Class

  Step 1 Locate 10 on the diagram.

  Step 2 Count the number of ✗'s above the number 10.

There are 4 students who are 10 years old.

For 1–4, use the line plot above.

1. There are _____ students who are 11 years old.

2. The same number of students are _____ and _____ years old.

3. The **range** is the difference between the greatest and least numbers in a set of data. The range in ages of students in the class is _____.

4. The **mode** is the number that occurs most often in a set of data. The number on the line plot with the most ✗'s is 9. So, the **mode** for this data is _____.

5. After the first morning of cartooning class, the students counted the number of cartoon pages they had completed. Use the data in the table to complete line plot.

CARTOON PAGES COMPLETED					
Number of Pages	2	3	4	5	6
Number of Students	2	4	7	2	1

2 3 4 5 6
Cartoon Pages Completed

Name _____

LESSON 15.5

Locate Points on a Grid

The horizontal and vertical lines in the square form a **grid**. An **ordered pair** of numbers such as (2,3) helps you find places on a grid. The numbers tell you how many places to move to the right of zero and how many to move up.

Locate the point (2,3) on the grid.

- Start at zero and move two spaces to the right.
- From that point, move up three spaces.

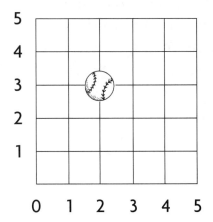

Look at each ordered pair. Name the sporting equipment you find at the point named by the ordered pair.

1. (3,1) _____
2. (1,2) _____
3. (4,4) _____
4. (5,6) _____
5. (6,2) _____
6. (2,3) _____
7. (7,5) _____
8. (1,6) _____
9. (5,1) _____
10. (2,5) _____

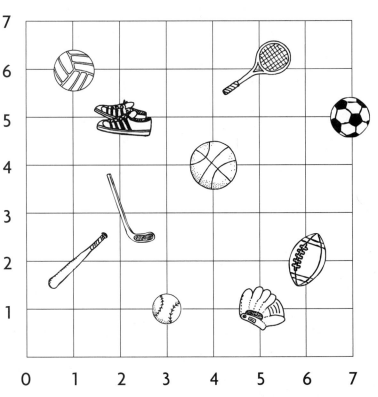

Reteach **RW77**

Name _____

LESSON 15.6

Read Line Graphs

Mr. King made this line graph to show the number of bicycles he sold each month for the first seven months of the year. This **line graph** shows how bike sales change over time.

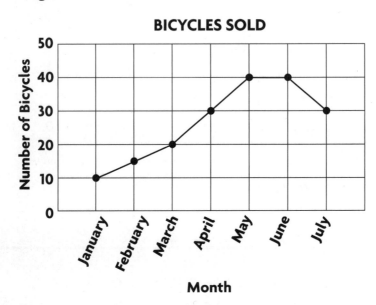

How many bicycles were sold in April?

Step 1 Find the line labeled April. Put your finger on the line. Follow that line up to the point (•).

Step 2 Move your finger along the line to the left to locate the number of bicycles sold in April.

Mr. King sold 30 bicycles during April.

For 1–4, use the graph above.

1. Mr. King sold the greatest number of bicycles during

   _____ and _____.

2. During March, Mr. King sold _____ bicycles.

3. During February, Mr. King sold _____ bicycles.

4. Mr. King sold _____ more bicycles in June than in January.

RW78 Reteach

Name _____

LESSON 16.1

Certain and Impossible

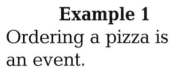

Example 1
Ordering a pizza is an event.

An **event** is something that happens.

Example 2
Ice cream melts when it gets hot. That is certain.

An event is **certain** if it will always happen.

Example 3
You will see an elephant fly. That is impossible.

An event is **impossible** if it will never happen.

Tell whether each event is *certain* or *impossible*.

1. When food comes out of the hot oven, it is hot.

2. Ice cubes will melt in the freezer.

3. It is cold outside when it snows.

4. December is the month after November.

5. You can swim on the grass.

6. You ice-skate on ice.

7. You will pick a blue marble from a bag filled with yellow and orange marbles.

8. If you stand out in the rain without an umbrella, you will get wet.

9. The dog will need water.

10. The Earth is round.

Reteach **RW79**

Name _____

LESSON 16.2

Likely and Unlikely

Look at the spinner.

Is spinning a number with 2 as a digit a *likely* or an *unlikely* event?

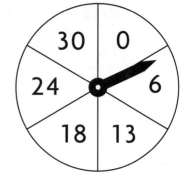

- How many parts have a number with 2 as a digit? _____

- How many parts do not have a number with 2 as a digit? _____

Compare. 1 < 5 so, spinning a number with 2 as a digit is unlikely.

For 1–4, look at the spinner. Write *likely* or *unlikely* for each event.

1. a number greater than zero

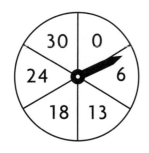

_____

2. a number greater than 15

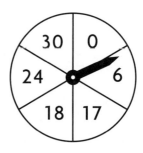

_____

3. a number less than 10

_____

4. a 2-digit number

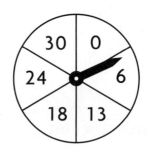

_____

RW80 Reteach

Name _____

LESSON 16.3

Possible Outcomes

A **possible outcome** is something that has a chance of happening. If you spin the pointer of the spinner at the right, the two possible outcomes are A and B.

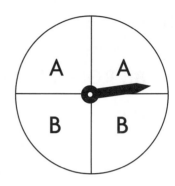

Two outcomes are **equally likely** if they have the same chance of happening. On this spinner, spinning an A has the same chance of happening as spinning a B.

The chance of spinning an A is 2 out of 4.

For 1-4, list the possible outcomes of each event.

1. using this spinner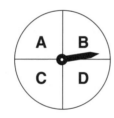

   _____

2. pulling marbles from this bag

   _____

3. tossing a bean bag on this gameboard

   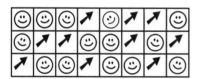

   _____

4. pulling a number from this bag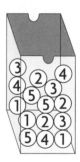

   _____

5. Bennie used this spinner. The pointer landed 2 times on A, and 1 time on B. Predict the letter it will land on next. What is the chance he will spin C?

   _____

Reteach RW81

Name _____

LESSON 16.4

Experiments

When you try an experiment, recording the results in a tally table helps you organize the information.

CUBE ROLL EXPERIMENT

Juan rolls the number cube 6 times.

- Record the results. Use one tally mark to show each result.
- Read the results.

Look at the tally table. A 3 is rolled three times, a 1 is rolled two times, and a 4 is rolled one time.

CUBE ROLL EXPERIMENT	
Number Rolled	Tallies
1	//
3	///
4	/

For Exercises 1–4, read the following experiment.

Anita and Kim put 30 stickers in a bag. There were heart, star, and clown stickers. Anita and Kim pulled 15 stickers out of the bag. Look at the tally table to see the results.

1. Which sticker was pulled most often?

   _____

2. Which sticker was pulled least often?

   _____

3. Why do you think one sticker was pulled more than the others?

STICKER EXPERIMENT	
Sticker	Tallies
Heart	////
Clown	//
Star	̶H̶̶H̶̶T̶ ////

_____

4. Do you think the results would be different if they did the experiment again?

_____

_____

Name _____

LESSON 16.5

Predict Outcomes

Experiments can help you predict outcomes.

Example: Students recorded what was served in the school cafeteria every Friday for 8 weeks. What could they predict will most likely be served in the cafeteria the next Friday?

FRIDAY LUNCHES	
Meal	Tallies
Pizza	ЖЖ
Spaghetti	//
Soup	/

Solution: Since there were more Fridays on which pizza was served, it is most likely that pizza will be served the next Friday in the cafeteria.

For 1–4, write your prediction for each problem.

1. These tallies show the pulls from a bag of color tiles. Predict which color is *least likely* to be pulled.

   red   Ж ////
   green   Ж Ж Ж //
   yellow   ///

   _____

2. This line plot shows the results of rolling a cube. Predict which number you would most likely roll.

   ```
   X
   X
   X
   X
   X         X         X
   X         X         X
   +--+--+--+--+--+--+
   1  2  3  4  5  6
   ```

   _____

3. These tallies show the results of tossing a coin. Predict whether the coin will land *heads* or *tails* on the next toss.

   heads   Ж Ж /
   tails   Ж Ж /

   _____
   _____

4. These tallies show the pulls from a bag of marbles. Predict which color marble is most likely to be pulled.

   red   Ж /
   green   Ж Ж Ж Ж
   purple   Ж /

   _____

5. This line plot shows the results of spinning an A, B, C, or D on a spinner. Predict which letter is *least likely* to be landed on. _____

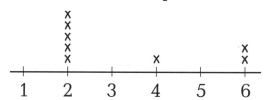

Reteach   **RW83**

Name _____

Problem Solving Skill: Draw Conclusions

You can decide if a spinner is fair or unfair.

Example 1

Tusu spins the pointer to see where his game piece should move on the game board. He has the same chance of spinning each color because the parts are the same size and there are the same number of parts for each color.

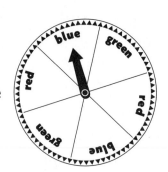

Example 2

Sheila spins the pointer to see where her game piece should move on the game board. She does not have the same chance of spinning each color because the blue parts are larger than the parts of any other colors.

When you play a game, it is **fair** if all of the outcomes have an equal chance of happening.

For 1–4, tell which item is fair. Write A or B.

1. 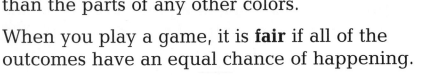 _____

2. _____

3. 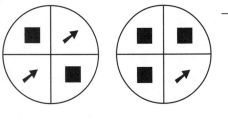 _____

4. 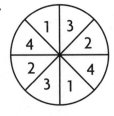 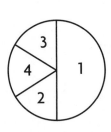 _____

5. What makes the items fair? _____

RW84 Reteach

Name _____

LESSON 17.1

Multiply 2-Digit Numbers

You can use grid paper to help you multiply.

Example 3 × 12

- Draw a rectangle with 3 rows and 12 columns on grid paper.

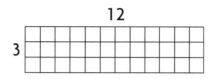

- Draw a line after the tenth column to make two rectangles.

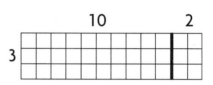

- There are 3 rows of 10.   3 × 10 = 30
- There are 3 rows of 2.   3 × 2 = 6
- There are 36 squares in all.   30 + 6 = 36
- So, 3 × 12 = 36

---

1. Use grid paper to model 4 × 11.

    a. How many rows of 10 are there? _____

    b. How many rows of 1 are there? _____

    c. How many squares are there in all? _____

    d. What is 4 × 11? _____

2. Use grid paper to model 5 × 13.

    a. How many rows of 10 are there? _____

    b. How many rows of 3 are there? _____

    c. How many squares are there in all? _____

    d. What is 5 × 13? _____

3. Use grid paper to find 6 × 18. _____

Reteach RW85

Name _____

LESSON 17.2

Record Multiplication

Example 24
         × 3

- Multiply the ones.
  3 × 4 ones = 12 ones

- Multiply the tens.
  3 × 2 tens = 6 tens

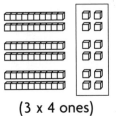 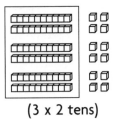
(3 × 4 ones)   (3 × 2 tens)

```
   24
 ×  3
   12   ← 3 x 4 ones
 + 60   ← 3 x 2 tens
   72   ← total
```

- Record the products under the original problem.

- Add the two products.

Find the product. You may wish to use base-ten blocks.

1. 13
   × 2
   ____ ← product of ones
 + ____ ← product of tens
   ____

2. 23
   × 4
   ____ ← product of ones
 + ____ ← product of tens
   ____

3. 15
   × 3
   ____ ← product of ones
 + ____ ← product of tens
   ____

4. 16
   × 5
   ____ ← product of ones
 + ____ ← product of tens
   ____

5. 12
   × 3
   ____ ← product of ones
 + ____ ← product of tens
   ____

6. 22
   × 5
   ____ ← product of ones
 + ____ ← product of tens
   ____

7. 32
   × 4

8. 25
   × 4

9. 36
   × 5

Name _____

LESSON 17.3

Practice Multiplication

Example   38
      × 4

- Multiply the ones.
  4 × 8 ones = 32 ones

- Regroup 32 ones as 3 tens 2 ones.

- Write the 2 in the ones column and the 3 above the tens.

Hundreds	Tens	Ones
	3	
	3	8
×		4
		2

- Multiply the tens.
  4 × 3 tens = 12 tens

- Add the 3 tens you regrouped.
  12 + 3 tens = 15 tens

- Regroup 15 tens as 1 hundred 5 tens.

- Write the 5 in the tens column and the 1 in the hundreds column.

Hundreds	Tens	Ones
	3	
	3	8
×		4
1	5	2

Find the product. You may use base-ten blocks to help you.

1. 18
   × 3

2. 36
   × 2

3. 55
   × 5

4. 61
   × 4

5. 27
   × 4

6. 14
   × 7

7. 32
   × 6

8. 17
   × 2

9. 12
   × 8

10. 63
   × 6

11. 45
   × 4

12. 52
   × 5

Reteach   RW87

Problem Solving Skill: Choose the Operation

Multiply:
- when you are joining equal groups.
- when you know the size of the equal groups and the number of groups.

Example: Josh has 4 decks of playing cards. Each deck has 52 cards. How many cards does Josh have in all?

$4 \times 52 = 208$

Josh has 208 cards.

Divide:
- when you are separating a total into equal groups.
- when you know the total and the number of groups.

Example: There are 4 children who are sharing a bag of 32 crackers. How many crackers does each child get?

$32 \div 4 = 8$

Each child gets 8 crackers.

Write whether you would *add*, *subtract*, *multiply*, or *divide*. Then solve.

1. Mr. Davis drives 26 miles each day. How many miles does he drive in 5 days?

2. Felix baked 48 cookies for a bake sale. Jane baked 36 cookies. How many cookies did they bake in all?

3. Mrs. Watkins wants to buy a pair of skates. She has $50 and the skates cost $29. How much money will she get back in change?

4. Maria read 45 pages in 5 days. She read the same number of pages daily. How many pages did she read each day?

5. There are 21 students riding in 3 vans. The same number of students are riding in each van. How many students are in each van?

6. There are 3 classes visiting the library. There are 26 students in each class. How many students are visiting the library in all?

Name _____ LESSON 18.1

Mental Math: Patterns in Multiplication

You can use place-value patterns to help you multiply by tens, hundreds, and thousands. Look at the number sentences below. Count the number of zeros in the second factor. Then count the number of zeros in the product.

$$5 \times 1 = 5 \qquad 2 \times 3 = 6$$
$$5 \times 10 = 50 \qquad 2 \times 30 = 60$$
$$5 \times 100 = 500 \qquad 2 \times 300 = 600$$
$$5 \times 1{,}000 = 5{,}000 \qquad 2 \times 3{,}000 = 6{,}000$$

Complete. Use patterns and mental math to help.

1. $8 \times 1 =$ _____
   $8 \times 10 =$ _____
   $8 \times 100 =$ _____
   $8 \times 1{,}000 =$ _____

2. $4 \times 3 =$ _____
   $4 \times 30 =$ _____
   $4 \times 300 =$ _____
   $4 \times 3{,}000 =$ _____

3. $5 \times 3 =$ _____
   _____ $\times 30 = 150$
   $5 \times$ _____ $= 1{,}500$
   $5 \times 3{,}000 =$ _____

4. $4 \times 5 =$ _____
   _____ $\times 50 = 200$
   $4 \times$ _____ $= 2{,}000$
   $4 \times 5{,}000 =$ _____

Use mental math and basic facts to solve.

5. $9 \times 60 =$ _____
6. $7 \times$ _____ $= 35{,}000$
7. _____ $\times 40 = 160$
8. $6 \times$ _____ $= 4{,}200$
9. $2 \times$ _____ $= 14{,}000$
10. _____ $\times 300 = 900$
11. _____ $\times 50 = 450$
12. _____ $\times 90 = 810$
13. $4 \times 9{,}000 =$ _____
14. $2 \times 500 =$ _____
15. $8 \times 400 =$ _____
16. $7 \times$ _____ $= 490$
17. _____ $\times 800 = 6{,}400$
18. $2 \times 8{,}000 =$ _____
19. $3 \times 700 =$ _____
20. $6 \times 30 =$ _____
21. $4 \times 100 =$ _____
22. $3 \times 900 =$ _____

Reteach

Name _____

LESSON 18.2

Problem Solving Strategy: Find a Pattern

You can *find a pattern* and use basic facts to solve some problems.

Read the following problem.

A theater shows 6 movies at one time. There are enough seats for 200 people to see each movie. How many people can be seated at one time in the theater?

1. Underline what you are asked to find.

2. What information will you use? _____
   _____
   _____

3. What strategy can you use to solve the problem?
   _____

4. How can you use the strategy to solve the problem?
   _____
   _____
   _____

5. Solve the problem.
   _____

Find a pattern to solve.

6. The Journal News sells 600 newspapers each day. How many newspapers does it sell in 7 days?

   _____

7. A builder uses 400 pounds of lumber to build a shed. If the builder builds 9 sheds, how many pounds of lumber will he use?

   _____

8. A zoo feeds 300 pounds of food to its animals each day. How many pounds of food does the zoo feed in 8 days?

   _____

9. An airline flies 5,000 people each day. How many people does it fly in 6 days?

   _____

RW90 Reteach

Name _____

LESSON 18.3

Estimate Products

You can estimate products when you don't need an exact number.

$$32 \times 6 = \underline{} \text{ or } \begin{array}{r} 32 \\ \times 6 \\ \hline \end{array}$$

Remember
To round a number:
- Decide on the place to be rounded.
- Look at the digit to its right.
- If the digit is less than 5, the digit being rounded stays the same.
- If the digit is 5 or more, the digit being rounded increases by 1.

Step 1
Round the first factor to the greatest place value.

$$\begin{array}{r} 32 \\ \times 6 \\ \hline \end{array} \rightarrow \begin{array}{r} 30 \\ \times 6 \\ \hline \end{array}$$

Step 2
Multiply.

$$\begin{array}{r} 30 \\ \times 6 \\ \hline 180 \end{array}$$

Estimate the product.

1. $\begin{array}{r} 38 \\ \times 7 \\ \hline \end{array} \rightarrow \begin{array}{r} 40 \\ \times 7 \\ \hline \end{array}$

2. $\begin{array}{r} 81 \\ \times 3 \\ \hline \end{array} \rightarrow$

3. $\begin{array}{r} 79 \\ \times 5 \\ \hline \end{array} \rightarrow$

4. $\begin{array}{r} 614 \\ \times 9 \\ \hline \end{array} \rightarrow$

5. $\begin{array}{r} 278 \\ \times 7 \\ \hline \end{array} \rightarrow$

6. $\begin{array}{r} 792 \\ \times 4 \\ \hline \end{array} \rightarrow$

7. $\begin{array}{r} 54 \\ \times 7 \\ \hline \end{array} \rightarrow$

8. $\begin{array}{r} 24 \\ \times 8 \\ \hline \end{array} \rightarrow$

9. $\begin{array}{r} 39 \\ \times 3 \\ \hline \end{array} \rightarrow$

10. $\begin{array}{r} 561 \\ \times 2 \\ \hline \end{array} \rightarrow$

11. $\begin{array}{r} 835 \\ \times 4 \\ \hline \end{array} \rightarrow$

12. $\begin{array}{r} 77 \\ \times 8 \\ \hline \end{array} \rightarrow$

13. $\begin{array}{r} 63 \\ \times 9 \\ \hline \end{array} \rightarrow$

14. $\begin{array}{r} 54 \\ \times 6 \\ \hline \end{array} \rightarrow$

15. $\begin{array}{r} 94 \\ \times 3 \\ \hline \end{array} \rightarrow$

Reteach RW91

Name _____

LESSON 18.4

Multiply 3-Digit Numbers

When you multiply 3-digit numbers, you multiply the ones, the tens, and then the hundreds and regroup when needed.

$$157 \times 3 = \underline{\ ?\ } \text{ or } \begin{array}{r} 157 \\ \times\ 3 \\ \hline \end{array} \qquad \text{Estimate. } 200 \times 3 = 600.$$

Step 1
Multiply the ones.
3 × 7 ones = 21 ones
Regroup 21 ones as 2 tens 1 one.

hundreds	tens	ones
	2	
1	5	7
×		3
		1

Step 2
Multiply the tens.
3 × 5 tens = 15 tens
15 tens + 2 tens = 17 tens. Regroup 17 tens as 1 hundred 7 tens.

hundreds	tens	ones
1	2	
1	5	7
×		3
	7	1

Step 3
Multiply the hundreds.
3 × 1 hundred = 3 hundreds. 3 hundreds + 1 hundred = 4 hundreds.

hundreds	tens	ones
1	2	
1	5	7
×		3
4	7	1

157 × 3 = 471

Multiply. Tell in which place you need to regroup.

1. 216
   × 4

2. 338
   × 5

3. 281
   × 3

4. 813
   × 2

5. 530
   × 5

Find the product. Estimate to check.

6. 415
   × 9

7. 652
   × 7

8. 184
   × 2

9. 436
   × 3

10. 925
   × 4

11. 138
   × 6

12. 747
   × 5

13. 842
   × 8

14. 342
   × 5

15. 259
   × 6

RW92 Reteach

Name _____

LESSON 18.5

Find Products Using Money

Multiply money amounts the same way you multiply whole numbers. Then write the product in dollars and cents.

$2.54 × 3 = __?__ or $2.54 × 3   Estimate. $3.00 × 3 = $9.00.

Step 1
Write the problem using whole numbers.

$2.54   →   254
×   3   ×   3

Step 2
Multiply to find the product.

  1 1
  2 5 4
×   3
─────────
  7 6 2

Step 3
Write the product in dollars and cents.

$7.62
Since $7.62 is close to $9.00, the answer is reasonable.

Find the product in dollars and cents. Estimate to check.

1. $3.46 × 7
2. $8.38 × 3
3. $5.81 × 4
4. $2.50 × 5
5. $4.35 × 2

6. $6.15 × 9
7. $7.52 × 4
8. $3.84 × 3
9. $5.12 × 6
10. $8.35 × 4

11. $9.38 × 5
12. $2.47 × 4
13. $6.42 × 8
14. $7.25 × 7
15. $2.81 × 3

16. $1.57 × 7
17. $8.75 × 3
18. $6.25 × 7
19. $3.54 × 4
20. $3.92 × 8

Reteach **RW93**

Name _____

LESSON 18.6

Practice Multiplication

You can multiply 4-digit numbers the same way you multiply 2- and 3-digit numbers.

$$2{,}354 \times 4 = \underline{\;?\;} \text{ or } \begin{array}{r} 2{,}354 \\ \times \quad\quad 4 \\ \hline \end{array}$$

Estimate. $2{,}000 \times 4 = 8{,}000$.

Step 1
Multiply the ones. Regroup if needed.

Step 2
Multiply the tens. Regroup if needed.

Step 3
Multiply the hundreds. Regroup if needed.

Step 4
Multiply the thousands.

Th	H	T	O
		1	
2,	3	5	4
×			4
			6

Th	H	T	O
	2	1	
2,	3	5	4
×			4
		1	6

Th	H	T	O
1	2	1	
2,	3	5	4
×			4
	4	1	6

Th	H	T	O
1	2	1	
2,	3	5	4
×			4
9,	4	1	6

$2{,}354 \times 4 = 9{,}416$

Find the product. Estimate to check.

1. 1,346 × 5
2. $18.58 × 2
3. 3,781 × 3
4. 4,315 × 7
5. 7,152 × 4

6. 3,594 × 3
7. $19.28 × 6
8. 247 × 5
9. 3,042 × 8
10. $43.57 × 4

11. 1,904 × 6
12. 4,267 × 7
13. 5,530 × 4
14. 6,537 × 2
15. $25.93 × 5

RW94 Reteach

Name _____

LESSON 19.1

Divide with Remainders

Sometimes you cannot divide objects evenly into groups.

Find 14 ÷ 4.

Use 14 counters.

Draw 4 circles. Divide the 14 counters into 4 equal groups by putting the same number of counters into each circle.

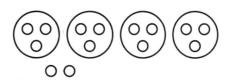

The **quotient** is 3—the number of counters in each of the 4 groups.
The **remainder** is 2—the number of leftover counters.

Write: 14 ÷ 4 = 3 r2

Use the picture to find the quotient and remainder.

1. 11 ÷ 2 = _____   (ooooo)(ooooo) o

2. 9 ÷ 4 = _____   (oo)(oo)(oo)(oo) o

3. 13 ÷ 3 = _____   (oooo)(oooo)(oooo) o

4. 11 ÷ 4 = _____   (oo)(oo)(oo)(oo) o o o

Find the quotient and remainder. You may use counters to help.

5. 12 ÷ 5 = _____   6. 10 ÷ 3 = _____   7. 9 ÷ 2 = _____

8. 13 ÷ 2 = _____   9. 15 ÷ 4 = _____   10. 8 ÷ 3 = _____

11. 10 ÷ 4 = _____   12. 7 ÷ 3 = _____   13. 17 ÷ 3 = _____

14. 11 ÷ 3 = _____   15. 16 ÷ 5 = _____   16. 5 ÷ 3 = _____

Reteach RW95

Name _____

LESSON 19.2

Model Division of 2-Digit Numbers

Divide 74 into 3 equal groups.

Write: 74 ÷ 3 = ■

Step 1	Step 2
Show 74 as 7 tens and 4 ones. 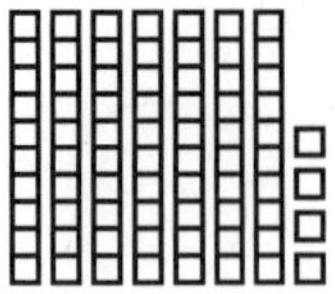 Draw 3 circles to show 3 groups. 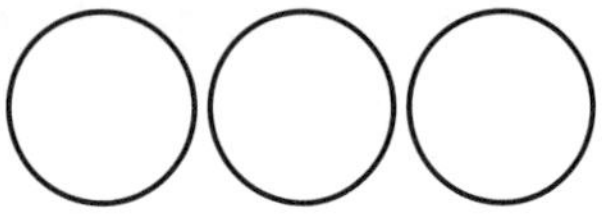	Begin by dividing the 7 tens. Place an equal number of tens into each group. 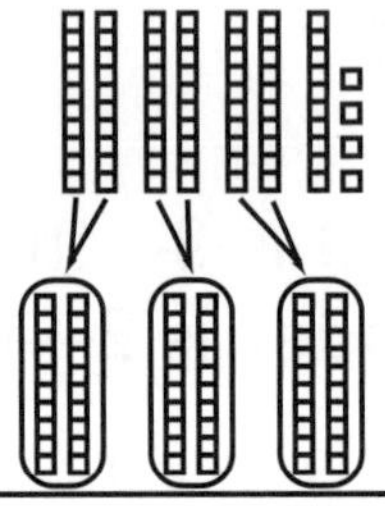
Step 3	**Step 4**
There are now 2 tens in each group. Regroup the 1 ten left over into ones. Now there are 14 ones. 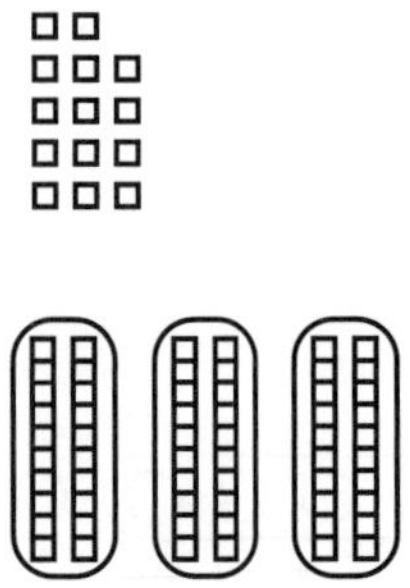	Divide the 14 ones. Place an equal number of ones in each group. 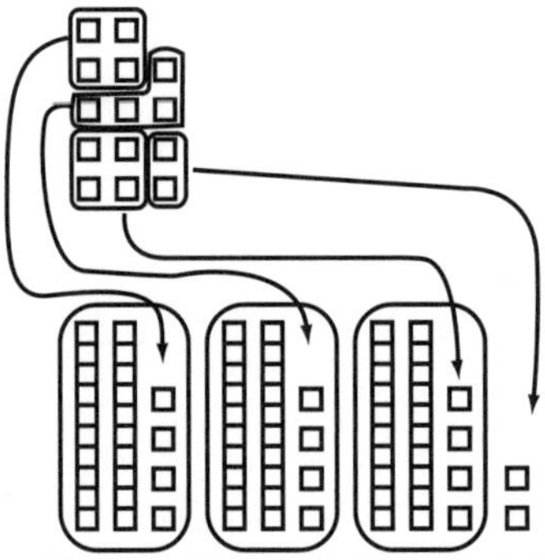

There are 2 tens and 4 ones in each group. There are 2 ones left over.

So, 74 ÷ 3 = 24 r2.

Divide. Use base-ten blocks to model each problem.

1. 35 ÷ 2 = _____
2. 35 ÷ 3 = _____
3. 35 ÷ 4 = _____

4. 67 ÷ 2 = _____
5. 67 ÷ 3 = _____
6. 67 ÷ 4 = _____

7. 45 ÷ 2 = _____
8. 45 ÷ 3 = _____
9. 45 ÷ 4 = _____

RW96 Reteach

Name _____

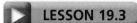
LESSON 19.3

Record Division of 2-Digit Numbers

Divide 93 into 4 equal groups.

Write: 93 ÷ 4 = ▪ and 4)93

Step 1	Step 2
Show 93 as 9 tens and 3 ones. Draw 4 circles to show 4 groups.	Begin by dividing the 9 tens. Place an equal number of tens into each group. 2 ← 2 tens in each group $4)93$ -8 ← 8 tens used 1 ← 1 ten left

Step 3	Step 4	Step 5
Regroup the 1 ten left over into ones. Now there are 13 ones. 2 $4)93$ $-8↓$ 13 ← bring down ones	Divide the 13 ones. Place an equal number of ones in each group. 23 ← 3 ones in each group $4)93$ $-8↓$ 13 -12 ← 12 ones used 1 ← 1 one left	Record the remainder next to the quotient. $23\ r1$ $4)93$ $-\ 8$ 13 -12 1

So, 93 ÷ 4 = 23 r1 and $4\overline{)93}$ with quotient 23 r1.

Use base-ten blocks to model each problem. Record the numbers as you complete each step.

1. $2\overline{)49}$ 2. $3\overline{)52}$ 3. $4\overline{)51}$ 4. $2\overline{)71}$

Reteach RW97

Name _____

 LESSON 19.4

Practice Division

63 ÷ 4 = ■

Remember these steps:
Divide
Multiply
Subtract
Compare
Bring down

1 $4\overline{)63}$ $\underline{-4}$ 2	**Divide the tens** **Multiply** 4 × 1 = 4 **Subtract** 6 − 4 = 2 **Compare** 2 < 4
1 $4\overline{)63}$ $\underline{-4\downarrow}$ 23	**Bring down the ones**
15 $4\overline{)63}$ $\underline{-4\downarrow}$ 23 $\underline{-20}$ 3	**Divide the ones** **Multiply** 4 × 5 = 20 **Subtract** 23 − 20 = 3 **Compare** 3 < 4
$15\text{ r}3$ $4\overline{)63}$ $\underline{-4\downarrow}$ 23 $\underline{-20}$ 3	**Bring down?** There is nothing left to bring down. If there is a remainder, record it next to the quotient.

Find the quotient. Use the D, M, S, C, and B steps above.

1. $2\overline{)73}$ 2. $5\overline{)60}$ 3. $4\overline{)66}$ 4. $3\overline{)75}$

Name _____

LESSON 20.2

Estimate Quotients

When you don't need an exact answer, you can estimate to find the quotient.

$132 \div 4 = \blacksquare$ or $4\overline{)132}$

Step 1	**Step 2**	**Step 3**
Look at the first two digits.	Think of a basic fact that is close to that number.	Then use a pattern to estimate.
$132 \div 4 = \blacksquare$	$12 \div 4 = 3$	$12 \div 4 = 3$ $120 \div 4 = 30$

Estimate each quotient. Write the basic fact you used to find the estimate.

1. $155 \div 5 = \blacksquare$ 2. $334 \div 8 = \blacksquare$ 3. $205 \div 4 = \blacksquare$

  _____   _____   _____

4. $736 \div 9 = \blacksquare$ 5. $629 \div 7 = \blacksquare$ 6. $745 \div 8 = \blacksquare$

  _____   _____   _____

7. $2\overline{)112}$ 8. $6\overline{)419}$ 9. $4\overline{)338}$

  _____   _____   _____

10. $9\overline{)378}$ 11. $6\overline{)117}$ 12. $9\overline{)531}$

  _____   _____   _____

Estimate the quotient.

13. $325 \div 6 =$ _____ 14. $238 \div 5 =$ _____ 15. $271 \div 3 =$ _____

16. $2\overline{)172}$ 17. $7\overline{)352}$ 18. $3\overline{)284}$

Reteach **RW101**

Name _____

LESSON 20.3

Place the First Digit in the Quotient

When you divide, you must decide where to place the first digit in the quotient.

$$174 \div 3 = \blacksquare \text{ or } 3\overline{)174}$$

Step 1

Decide where to place the first digit in the quotient.

$3\overline{)174}$ 1 < 3, so look at the tens.

$3\overline{)\mathbf{174}}$ 17 > 3, so use 17 tens. Place the first digit in the tens place.

So, 174 ÷ 3 = 58.

Step 2

Divide the 17 tens by 3.

```
       5
   3)174    Divide. 3)17
   -15      Multiply 3 × 5.
     2      Subtract 17 − 15.
            Compare. 2 < 3
            The difference
            must be less than
            the divisor.
```

Step 3

Bring down the 4 ones. Divide the 24 ones.

```
      58
   3)174
   -15↓
     24    Divide. 3)24
   - 24    Multiply 3 × 8.
      0    Subtract 24 − 24.
           Compare. 0 < 3
```

Place an X where the first digit in the quotient should be.

1. $3\overline{)252}$

2. $4\overline{)332}$

3. $7\overline{)203}$

Find the quotient.

4. $6\overline{)120}$

5. $9\overline{)333}$

6. $8\overline{)552}$

7. $2\overline{)156}$

8. $5\overline{)230}$

9. $3\overline{)96}$

Name _____

LESSON 20.4

Practice Division of 3-Digit Numbers

When you divide, you must decide where to place the first digit in the quotient.

$$576 \div 3 = \blacksquare \text{ or } 3\overline{)576}$$

Estimate: $600 \div 3 = 200$

Step 1

Decide where to place the first digit in the quotient.

$3\overline{)576}$ $5 > 3$, so divide the hundreds.

Step 2

Divide the 5 hundreds.

```
   1
3)576    Divide. 3)5
 -3      Multiply
  2      3 × 1.
         Subtract
         5 − 3.
         Compare.
         2 < 3
```

Step 3

Bring down the 7 tens.

```
   19
3)576    Divide. 3)27
 -3↓     Multiply
  27     3 × 9.
 -27     Subtract
   0     27 − 27.
         Compare.
         0 < 3
```

Step 4

Bring down the 6 ones.

```
   192
3)576    Divide. 3)6
 -3      Multiply
  27     3 × 2.
 -27     Subtract
  06     6 − 6.
   6     Compare.
   0     0 < 3
```

So, $576 \div 3 = 192$.

Find the quotient.

1. $6\overline{)738}$

2. $9\overline{)999}$

3. $3\overline{)372}$

4. $2\overline{)924}$

5. $5\overline{)240}$

6. $7\overline{)987}$

Reteach **RW103**

Name _____

LESSON 20.5

Divide Amounts of Money

You can divide money amounts like whole numbers. Place the dollar sign and the decimal point in the quotient.

$$\$4.59 \div 3 = \blacksquare \text{ or } 3\overline{)\$4.59}$$

Step 1
Divide the 4 hundreds.

```
  1
3)$4.59    3)4      Divide.
 -3                 Multiply
  1                 3 × 1.
                    Subtract
                    4 − 3.
                    Compare.
                    1 < 3
```

Step 2
Bring down the 5 tens.

```
   15
3)$4.59    3)15     Divide.
 -3↓                Multiply
   15               3 × 5.
  -15               Subtract
    0               15 − 15.
                    Compare.
                    0 < 3
```

Step 3
Bring down the 9 ones.

```
   153
3)$4.59    3)9      Divide.
 -3                 Multiply
   15               3 × 3.
  -15               Subtract
    09              9 − 9.
    -9              Compare.
     0              0 < 3
```

Step 4
Write the quotient with a dollar sign and a decimal point.

$$\$1.53$$
$$3)\$4.59$$

Find the quotient.

1. $5)\overline{\$7.35}$ 2. $3)\overline{\$9.39}$ 3. $4)\overline{\$3.72}$

4. $2)\overline{\$4.92}$ 5. $6)\overline{\$8.52}$ 6. $7)\overline{\$8.96}$

RW104 Reteach

Name _____

LESSON 20.6

Problem Solving Strategy
Solve a Simpler Problem

Read the following problem.

Lane Library is having its annual "Read-A-Book" day. There are 180 children signed up for the program. The children need to be placed into 3 groups. How many children will be in each group?

1. Underline what you are asked to find.

2. What information will you use?

   _____
   _____

3. What strategy can you use to solve the problem?

   _____

4. How can you use the strategy to solve the problem?

   _____
   _____

5. Solve the problem.

   _____

Use a simpler problem to solve.

6. Zach has $5.00 in nickels. How many nickels does he have?

   _____
   _____
   _____

7. Tanya has $20.00 in dimes. How many dimes does she have?

   _____
   _____
   _____

Reteach RW105

Name _____

LESSON 21.1

Solid Figures

These figures are called **solid figures.**

rectangular prism   cube   square pyramid   sphere   cone   cylinder

A **face** is a flat surface of a solid figure.

An **edge** is the line segment formed where two faces of a solid figure meet.

A **vertex** is a corner where 3 or more edges of a solid figure meet. Two or more corners are called *vertices*.

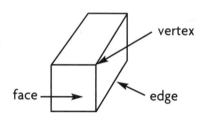

Name the solid figure each object looks like.

1.

2.

3.

4.

5.

6.

7.

8.

9.

RW106   Reteach

Name _____

LESSON 21.2

Combine Solid Figures

Solid figures an be combined to make different solid objects.

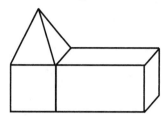 is made of and and  .

Name the solid figures used to make each object.

1.

2.

3.

_____   _____   _____

4.

5.

6.

_____   _____   _____

The objects in each pair should be the same. Name the solid figure that is missing.

7.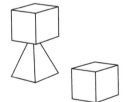

8.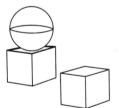

9.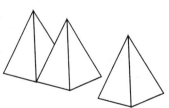

_____   _____   _____

10.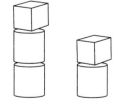

11.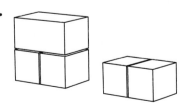

12.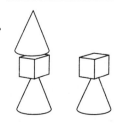

_____   _____   _____

Reteach **RW107**

Name _____

LESSON 21.3

Line Segments and Angles

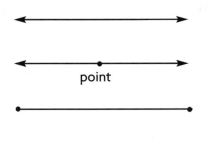

A **line** is straight. It continues in both directions. It does not end.

A **point** is an exact position or location.

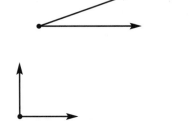

A **line segment** is straight. It is the part of a line between two points, called endpoints.

A **ray** is part of a line. It has one endpoint. It is straight and continues in one direction.

An **angle** is formed by two rays with the same endpoint.

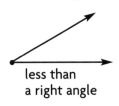
less than a right angle

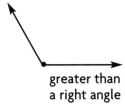
greater than a right angle

A **right angle** is a special angle. It forms a square corner.

Name each figure.

1. •
2. •———▶
3.
4. •———•

_____   _____   _____   _____

Write whether each angle is a *right angle*, *greater than* a right angle, or *less than* a right angle.

5.   6.    7.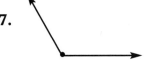

_____   _____   _____

8.   9.    10.

_____   _____   _____

RW108   Reteach

Name _____

LESSON 21.4

Types of Lines

Lines that cross each other are **intersecting lines.**
These lines intersect.

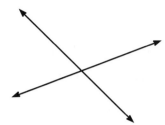

Lines that never cross are **parallel lines.** These lines are parallel.

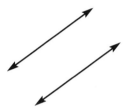

In 1–3, draw intersecting lines.

1. 2. 3.

For 4–5, use the map.

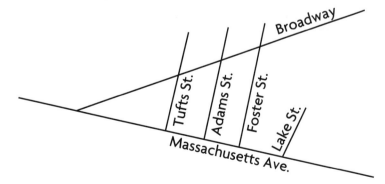

4. Name the streets parallel to Foster Street. _____

5. Name the streets that intersect Broadway.

_____

Name _____

LESSON 21.5

Circles

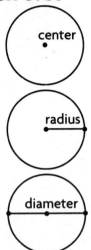

The **center** of a circle is the point in the middle of a circle. It is the same distance from anywhere on the circle.

A **radius** of a circle is a line segment. Its endpoints are the center of the circle and any point on the circle.

A **diameter** of a circle is a line segment. It passes through the center. Its endpoints are points on the circle.

For 1–4, use the circle at the right.

1. Draw a red point at the center of the circle.
2. Draw a blue radius.
3. Draw a green diameter.
4. Describe the angles formed by your diameter and radius.

   _____

   _____

   _____

For 5–8, use the circles at the right.

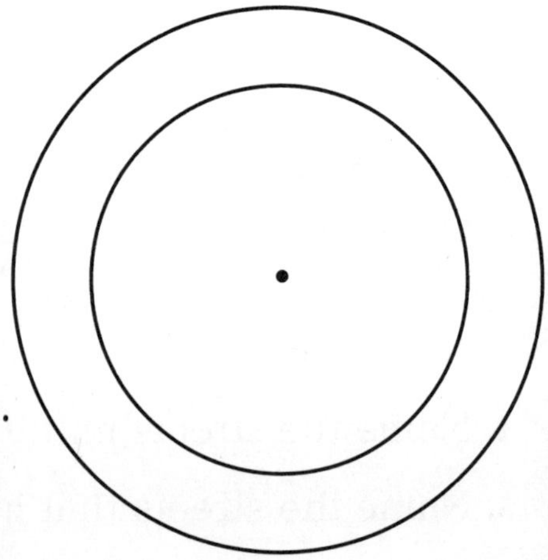

5. How are the circles alike?

   _____

   _____

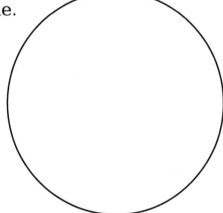

6. Draw a red radius on the larger circle.
7. Draw a green radius on the smaller circle.
8. How are the circles different?

   _____

   _____

RW110 Reteach

Name _____

> LESSON 21.6

Problem Solving Strategy
Break Problems into Simpler Parts

Donita paints designs on 8 children's cubes each day. Today she painted this pattern on each face of a cube. How many squares did Donita paint on the cube?

1. Underline what the problem asks.

2. What information will you use to answer the question?
   _____

3. Is there information you will not use? If so, what?
   _____

4. What strategy can you use to solve the problem?
   _____

5. How can you solve the problem?
   _____
   _____

6. There are _____ squares on one face.

7. There are _____ faces on the cube.

8. Solve the problem.
   _____
   _____

Solve each problem.

9. Donita painted this pattern on each side of a cube. How many circles did she paint?

   _____

10. Donita painted this pattern on each side of a cube. How many triangles did she paint in all?

    _____

Reteach RW111

Name _____

LESSON 22.1

Polygons

A **closed figure** begins and ends at the same point.

An **open figure** has ends that do not meet.

closed figures

open figure

A **polygon** is a closed figure with sides that are line segments. You can name and sort polygons by the number of sides or angles they have.

triangle	quadrilateral	pentagon	hexagon	octagon
3 sides 3 angles	4 sides 4 angles	5 sides 5 angles	6 sides 6 angles	8 sides 8 angles

---

Tell if each figure is a polygon. Write *yes* or *no*.

1. 2. 3. 4. 5.

_____   _____   _____   _____   _____

Write the number of sides and angles each polygon has. Then name the polygon.

6.   7.   8.   9.

_____   _____   _____   _____

_____   _____   _____   _____

_____   _____   _____   _____

RW112 Reteach

Name _____

LESSON 22.2

Congruence and Symmetry

Congruent figures have the same size and shape.

Examples

- Trace and cut out figure B in each example.
- Place figure B over figure A for each example.

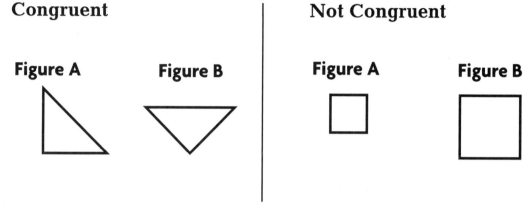

A **line of symmetry** is an imaginary line that divides a figure into 2 congruent parts. If you fold a figure along a line of symmetry, the two sides match, or are congruent. Some figures have 1 or more lines of symmetry. Some figures have no lines of symmetry.

Examples

X	E	P
2 lines of symmetry	1 line of symmetry	0 lines of symmetry

Tell whether the two figures are congruent. Write *yes* or *no*.

1.  2.  3.

_____ _____ _____

Draw the line or lines of symmetry on each figure.

4.   5.   6.   7.   8.

Reteach RW113

Name _____

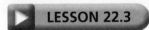

Combine Plane Figures

When you combine plane figures so that they cover a surface without overlapping or leaving a space between them, you are making a **tessellation**.

Not all figures tessellate.

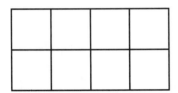

Tell if each figure will tessellate. Write *yes* or *no*.

1.   2. ⬭ 3.   4.

_____   _____   _____   _____

Use two different colors to make your own tessellation. Use the figure given.

5.

6.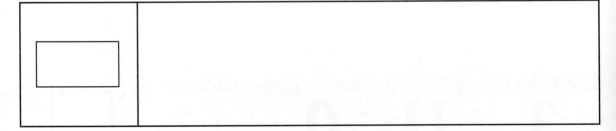

RW114 Reteach

Name _____

LESSON 22.4

Problem Solving Strategy

Find a Pattern

You can use the order of the shapes in a design to identify a pattern.

What shape comes next?
⊗ ○ ① ○ ⊗ ○ ① _?_ _?_

Every other figure is ○, so the next figure is ○.

The figures ⊗ and ① alternate, so the next figure is ⊗.
⊗ ○ ① ○ ⊗ ○ ① ○ ⊗

Draw the next two shapes in each pattern.

1.  ○ □ △ ○ □ △ ○ □ _____

2.  ⌂ △ △ ⌂ △ △ ⌂ △ _____

3.  ⌂ ⌬ □ □ ⌂ ⌬ □ □ _____

Draw the missing shapes in each pattern.

4. 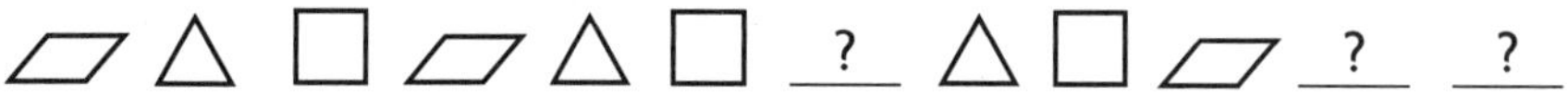 ▱ △ □ ▱ △ □ _?_ △ □ ▱ _?_ _?_ _____

5.  ⌂ △ ⌂ □ ⌂ △ ⌂ □ _?_ _?_ _?_ _____

6.  □ □ ⌂ △ □ □ ⌂ △ _?_ _?_ ⌂ _?_ _____

Reteach RW115

Name _____

LESSON 23.1

Triangles

Polygons with 3 sides and 3 angles are triangles.

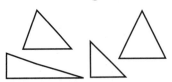
triangles

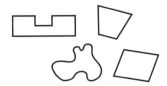
not triangles

You can describe any angle in a triangle as a *right angle*, *greater than* a right angle, or *less than* a right angle. Remember, a right angle forms a square corner.

EXAMPLES

greater than a right angle   less than a right angle   right angle

Write if each angle is a *right angle*, *greater than* a right angle, or *less than* a right angle.

1.   2.   3. 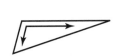   4.

_____   _____   _____   _____

_____   _____   _____   _____

5. 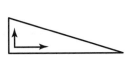   6.   7.   8.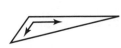

_____   _____   _____   _____

_____   _____   _____   _____

RW116   Reteach

Name _____

LESSON 23.2

Sort Triangles

You can name triangles by the number of equal sides they have.

equilateral   isosceles   scalene

All sides are equal.   Two sides are equal.   No sides are equal.

You can sort triangles by their angles.

right triangle

One right angle   one angle greater   three angles less
                   than a right angle   than a right angle

For 1–3, use the triangles at the right.
Write A, B, or C.

A   B   C

1. Which triangle is scalene? _____

2. Which triangles have at least 2 equal sides?

   _____

3. Which triangle has 3 angles less than a right triangle? _____

For 4–8, write one letter from each box to describe each triangle.

a. equilateral	d. It has 1 right angle.
b. isosceles	e. It has 1 angle greater than a right angle.
c. scalene	f. All angles are less than a right angle.

4.   5.   6.   7.   8.

_____ _____ _____ _____ _____

Reteach **RW117**

Name _____

LESSON 23.3

Quadrilaterals

Polygons with 4 sides and 4 angles are quadrilaterals.

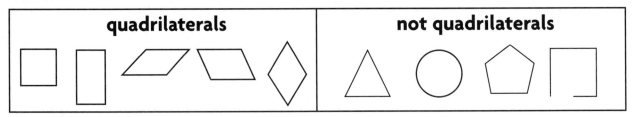

An angle in a quadrilateral can be a right angle, greater than a right angle, or less than a right angle. The sides of a quadrilateral can be parallel.

Examples

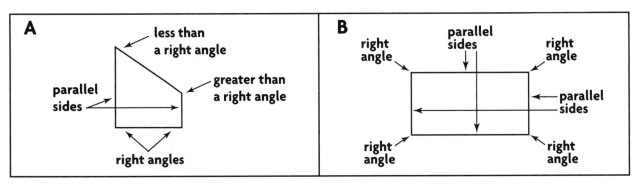

Describe the angles and sides of each quadrilateral.

1. _____

2. _____

3. _____

RW118 Reteach

Name _____

LESSON 23.4

Sort Quadrilaterals

There are special names for some kinds of quadrilaterals.

Parallelogram	Rhombus	Rectangle	Square
2 pairs of parallel sides 2 pairs of equal sides	2 pairs of parallel sides 4 equal sides	2 pairs of parallel sides 2 pairs of equal sides 4 right angles	2 pairs of parallel sides 4 equal sides 4 right angles

For 1–3, use the quadrilaterals at the right. Write A, B, C, D and E.

1. Which quadrilaterals have 2 pairs of parallel sides? _____

2. Which quadrilaterals have right angles? _____

3. How are quadrilaterals A and B alike? How are they different?

_____

_____

_____

For 4–7, write *all* the letters that describe each quadrilateral. Then write the name for each quadrilateral.

a. It has 4 equal sides.
b. It has 2 pairs of parallel sides.
c. It has 4 right angles.
d. It has 2 pairs of equal sides.

4. _____

5. _____

6. _____

7. _____

Reteach RW119

Name _____

LESSON 23.5

Problem Solving Skill

Identify Relationships

You can identify relationships among figures by comparing their characteristics.

Characteristics	Name
4 sides, 4 angles	quadrilateral
2 pairs of parallel sides	parallelogram
4 right angles	rectangle
4 equal sides	square
4 equal sides, no right angles	rhombus

Figure A has 4 sides, 4 angles, 2 pairs of parallel sides, and 4 right angles. It is a quadrilateral, a parallelogram, and a rectangle. The best name for this polygon is a rectangle.

1. What are all the ways to name the polygon at the right? What is the best name for the polygon?

_____

2. What are all the ways to name the polygon at the right? What is the best name for the polygon?

_____

For 3–4, use the figures at the right.

3. Choose the best names for the figures.

   A quadrilateral and square
   B parallelogram and rhombus
   C quadrilateral and rectangle
   D square and parallelogram

4. Which statement is not true?

   F They are quadrilaterals.
   G They are polygons.
   H They are triangles.
   J They are not squares.

RW120   Reteach

Name _____

Length

Sometimes you want to know **about** how long an object is.

You can use a ruler to measure an object.

- Line up one end of the object with the left end of the ruler.
- Look at the other end of the object.

Find the closest inch mark.	When you need a measurement that is more accurate, you can measure to the nearest half inch.
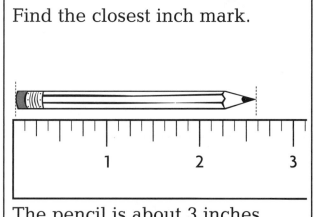	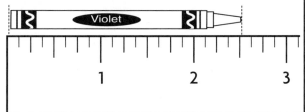
The pencil is about 3 inches long, to the nearest inch.	The crayon is about $2\frac{1}{2}$ inches long, to the nearest half inch.

Use a ruler to measure to the nearest inch.

Measure

1.    _____ in.

2. 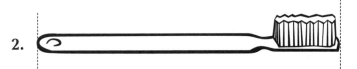   _____ in.

Use a ruler to measure the length to the nearest half inch.

3.    _____ in.

4.    _____ in.

Reteach RW121

Name _____

Inch, Foot, Yard, and Mile

The **inch (in.)**, **foot (ft)**, **yard (yd)**, and **mile (mi)** are customary units used to measure length or distance.

The length of a grasshopper is about 1 inch.

The length of Mr. Lee's boot is about 1 foot.

The height of Sara's little brother is about 1 yard.

The distance across Clear Lake is about 1 mile.

Complete each sentence. Write *more* or *less*.

1. The length of a jump rope is _____ than 1 foot.
2. The length of a paintbrush is _____ than 1 inch.
3. The distance you can throw a ball is _____ than 1 mile.
4. The length of a ladybug is _____ than 1 inch.
5. The length of a spoon is _____ than 1 yard.
6. The height of a goat is _____ than 1 foot.
7. The length of a classroom is _____ than 1 yard.
8. The distance around a city is _____ than 1 mile.

Choose the best unit to measure each item. Match by drawing a line.

9. the height of a door   inch
10. the distance around a football field   yard
11. the length of a carrot   mile
12. the distance between two towns   foot

Name _____

LESSON 24.3

Capacity

Capacity is the amount a container can hold.
Cup (c), **pint (pt)**, **quart (qt)**, and **gallon (gal)**
are customary units used to measure capacity.

2 cups = 1 pint   2 pints = 1 quart   4 quarts = 1 gallon

Circle the unit of measure that is greater.

1. cup   pint   2. gallon   quart   3. quart   pint

Complete each sentence. Write *more* or *less*.

4. A swimming pool contains _____ than 1 gallon.

5. A juice pitcher contains _____ than 1 cup.

6. A coffee mug contains _____ than 1 quart.

Circle the amount that is greater. Use the models above,
or make your own to help you.

7. 2 quarts   1 gallon

8. 4 cups   1 pint

9. 6 pints   1 quart

10. 2 cups   1 gallon

11. 4 pints   4 quarts

12. 6 quarts   1 gallon

Reteach   RW123

Name _____

LESSON 24.4

Weight

An **ounce (oz)** and a **pound (lb)** are customary units for measuring weight. Thinking about objects that weigh about 1 ounce or 1 pound can help you estimate the weight of other objects.

A large strawberry weighs about 1 ounce. A soccer ball weighs about 1 pound.

Complete each sentence. Write *more* or *less*.

1. A paper clip weighs _____ than 1 ounce.

2. A cat weighs _____ than 1 pound.

3. An apple weighs _____ than 1 ounce.

4. A sheet of paper weighs _____ than 1 ounce.

5. A watermelon weighs _____ than 1 pound.

6. A pencil weighs _____ than 1 pound.

Write the unit of measure you would use to weigh each object. Write *ounce* or *pound*.

7. 　　　8. 　　　9.

_____　　　_____　　　_____

10. 　　　11. 　　　12.

_____　　　_____　　　_____

RW124　Reteach

Name _____

LESSON 24.5

Ways to Change Units

To change from one unit of measure to another, you must know how the units are related.

Table of Measures		
Length	**Capacity**	
12 inches = 1 foot 3 feet = 1 yard	2 cups = 1 pint 2 pints = 1 quart 4 quarts = 1 gallon 4 cups = 1 quart 8 pints = 1 gallon	

How many cups are in 2 quarts?

1 quart   1 quart

1 quart = 4 cups

2 quarts = 4 + 4 or 8 cups

How many inches are in 3 feet?

1 foot   1 foot   1 foot

1 foot = 12 inches

2 feet = 12 + 12 or 24 inches

3 feet = 12 + 12 + 12 or 36 inches

Complete. Use the Table of Measures to help.

1. Change feet to inches.

    larger unit _____

    1 foot = _____

2. Change pints to quarts.

    larger unit _____

    1 quart = _____

Change the units. Use the Table of Measures to help.

3. _____ = 1 quart

    _____ = 4 quarts

4. _____ = 1 foot

    _____ = 4 feet

5. _____ = 1 gallon

pints	8	16	24	32
gallons	1	2	3	4

_____ = 4 gallons

6. _____ = 1 yard

feet	3	6	9	12
yards	1	2	3	4

_____ = 3 yards

Reteach   RW125

Name _____

LESSON 24.6

Algebra: Rules for Changing Units

You can use rules to help you change units.

Table of Measures	
Length 12 inches = 1 foot 3 feet = 1 yard	**Capacity** 2 cups = 1 pint 2 pints = 1 quart 4 quarts = 1 gallon 4 cups = 1 quart 8 pints = 1 gallon
To change a larger unit into a smaller unit, **multiply**. _?_ feet = 4 yards Think: 3 feet = 1 yard _?_ = 4 × 3 ____ feet = 4 yards	To change a smaller unit into a larger unit, **divide**. _?_ gallons = 32 pints Think: 8 pints = 1 gallon _?_ = 32 ÷ 8 ____ gallons = 32 pints

Complete. Use the Table of Measures to help.

1. ▨ feet = 8 yards   3 feet = 1 yard

    ▨ = 8 × 3

    ____ feet = 8 yards

2. ▨ gallons = 56 pints   8 pints = 1 gallon

    ▨ = 56 ÷ 8

    ____ gallons = 56 pints

3. ▨ yards = 9 feet   3 feet = 1 yard

    ▨ = 9 ÷ 3

    ____ yards = 9 feet

4. ▨ quarts = 10 gallons   4 qts. = 1 gal.

    ▨ = 10 × 4

    ____ quarts = 10 gallons

5. ▨ feet = 9 yards   3 feet = 1 yard

    ▨ = ____ × ____

    ____ feet = 9 yards

6. ▨ pints = 12 cups   2 cups = 1 pint

    ▨ = ____ ÷ ____

    ____ pints = 12 cups

RW126   Reteach

Name _____

LESSON 24.7

Problem Solving Skill

Use a Graph

You have used models, tables, and rules to change units of measurement. You can also use graphs to change units of measurement.

This bar graph shows the number of pints that are in quarts. Find the bar for 1 quart. The bar for 1 quart stops at the line for 2 pints. So, there are 2 pints in 1 quart.

You can also look for a pattern on the graph. When the number of quarts increases by 1, the number of pints increases by 2.

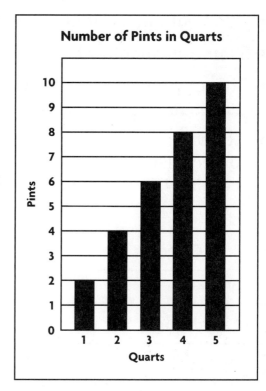

Use the graph above to answer questions.

1. How many pints are in 2 quarts? _____

2. How many quarts are in 10 pints? _____

3. How many pints are in 4 quarts? _____

4. If you had 6 pints of juice, how many quarts of juice would you have? _____

5. Complete the rule for changing quarts to pints.

   Multiply the number of quarts by _____.

Name _____

LESSON 25.1

Length

- The width of your index finger is about 1 **centimeter (cm)**.
- The width of an adult's hand is about 1 **decimeter (dm)**.
- Your arm span is about 1 **meter (m)**.
- Five city blocks is about 1 **kilometer (km)**.

1. Record the unit you would use to measure each object. Then measure the lengths to the nearest *centimeter, decimeter, meter,* or *kilometer*.

Object	Unit	Measurement
Sneaker		
Chalkboard		
Watch		
Classmate's finger		
Your classroom		
Crayon		
Classmate's height		

2. Order the items in your list from shortest to longest.

   _____

   _____

3. List 2 distances you would measure in kilometers.

   _____

   _____

RW128 Reteach

Name _____

LESSON 25.2

Problem Solving Strategy

Make a Table

Each student in Mr. Kinley's math class needs 300 centimeters of yarn to complete a project. If he has 5 students, how many meters of yarn does he need?

You can make a table to solve a problem. Remember: 100 centimeters = 1 meter.

Centimeters or Meters of Yarn Needed

Number of Students	Centimeters	Meters
1	300	3
2	600	6
3	900	9
4	1,200	12
5	1,500	15

Use the table to solve the problem.

1. Five students need 1,500 centimeters of yarn. So, 5 students need _____ meters of yarn.

Make a table to solve.

2. What if Mr. Kinley had 7 students? How many meters of yarn would he need?
   _____

3. What if Mr. Kinley had 10 students? How many meters of yarn would he need? _____

Martin drove 3 kilometers. How many meters did he drive?

4. Which table could you use to help solve the problem? _____

A
kilometers	1	2	3
meters	1,000	2,000	3,000

C
meters	1	2	3
decimeters	10	20	30

B
centimeters	100	200	300
meters	1	2	3

D
decimeters	1	2	3
centimeters	10	20	30

5. What is the solution to the problem? _____

6. Which table could you use to find how many decimeters are in 2 meters? How many decimeters equal 2 meters?

_____

Reteach RW129

Name _____

LESSON 25.3

Capacity: Liters and Milliliters

Capacity is the amount a container will hold when it is filled. Capacity can be measured using the metric units **milliliter (mL)** and **liter (L)**.

1,000 mL = 1 L

---

1. The soccer coach has 8 L of sports drink. He wants to pour the drink into bottles that hold 1,000 mL each. How many bottles does he need?

   a. How many milliliters equal 1 liter? _____

   b. How many milliliters equal 8 liters? _____

   c. How many groups of 1,000 mL are in 8 L? _____

   d. How many bottles does he need? _____

2. Roy needs to put 4 liters of juice into a cooler. He has containers that hold 500 mL. How many containers of juice should he put into the cooler?

   a. How many milliliters equal 1 liter? _____

   b. How many milliliters equal 4 liters? _____

   c. How many groups of 500 are in 4,000? _____

   d. How many containers of juice does he need? _____

3. Tanya needs to put 6,000 mL of water into a tub. How many 1 L jugs should she fill?

   a. How many milliliters equal 1 liter? _____

   b. How many groups of 1,000 are in 6,000 mL? _____

   c. How many liter containers should she fill? _____

RW130 Reteach

Name _____

LESSON 25.4

Mass: Grams and Kilograms

The metric units for measuring mass are **gram (g)** and **kilogram (kg)**.

   1,000 g = 1 kg

---

1. A box has a mass of 7 kg. What is the mass of the box in grams?

   a. How many grams equal 1 kilogram? _____

   b. What is the mass of the box in kilograms? _____

   c. How many grams equal 7 kg? _____

   d. What is the mass of the box in grams? _____

2. A stack of books has a mass of 9,000 grams. What is the mass of the books in kilograms?

   a. How many grams equal 1 kilogram? _____

   b. What is the mass of the books in grams? _____

   c. How many kilograms equal 9,000 grams? _____

   d. What is the mass of the books in kilograms? _____

3. A suitcase has a mass of 12,000 grams. What is the mass of the suitcase in kilograms?

   a. How many grams equal 1 kilogram? _____

   b. How many groups of 1,000 are in 12,000? _____

   c. How many kilograms equal 12,000 grams? _____

   d. What is the mass of the suitcase in kilograms? _____

Reteach   RW131

Name _____

LESSON 25.5

Measure Temperature

The customary unit for measuring temperature is **degrees Fahrenheit (°F)**.

The metric unit for measuring temperature is **degrees Celsius (°C)**.

Water freezes at 32°F, or 0°C. Water boils at 212°F, or 100°C. Room temperature is about 68°F, or 20°C.

Temperature can be compared by using subtraction.

80 − 72 = 8

So, 80°F is 8° warmer than 72°F.

---

1. Write the temperature in °F.

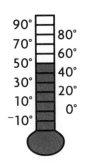

_____

2. Write the temperature in °C.

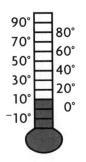

_____

3. Write the temperature in °F.

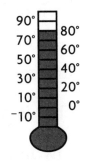

_____

Write the temperatures in °F. Find the difference between the temperatures.

4.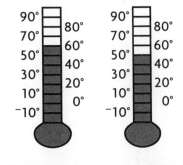

___   ___

_____

5.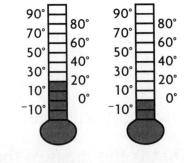

___   ___

_____

RW132 Reteach

Name _____

LESSON 26.1

Perimeter

Perimeter is the distance around a figure.

Jack used square tiles to measure the perimeter of a photograph of his cat. He needed 16 square tiles to go all the way around the photograph.

The perimeter of the photograph is 16 tiles.

Find the perimeter of each figure. You may use square tiles.

1.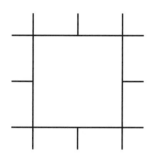

   _____

2.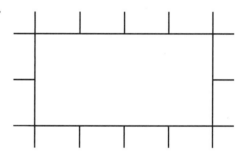

   _____

3.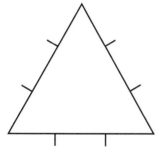

   _____

4.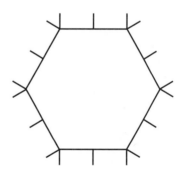

   _____

5.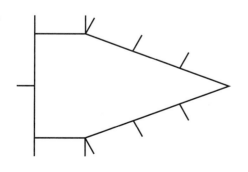

   _____

6.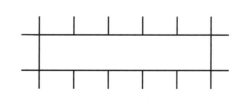

   _____

Reteach RW133

Name _____

LESSON 26.2

Estimate and Find Perimeter

Perimeter is the distance around a figure. You can add the lengths of the sides of a figure to find the perimeter.

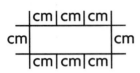
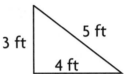

1 cm + 3 cm + 1 cm + 3 cm = 8 cm

3 ft + 4 ft + 5 ft = 12 ft

The perimeter is 8 centimeters.

The perimeter is 12 feet.

Use a centimeter ruler to measure the length of each side. Then add the lengths of the sides to find the perimeter.

1.

2.

_____

_____

3.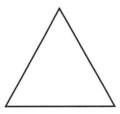

4.

_____

_____

Find the perimeter of each figure.

5.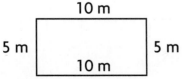

6.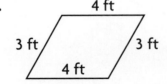

7.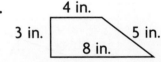

_____ _____ _____

RW134 Reteach

Name _____

Area of Plane Figures

The **area** of a figure is the number of square units needed to cover a flat surface.

This is a square unit. ☐   Count or skip-count the number of square units to find the area. The area of the figure is 6 square units.

Find the area of each figure. Write the area in square units.

1.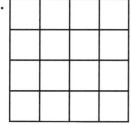

2.

3.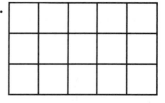

_____   _____   _____

4.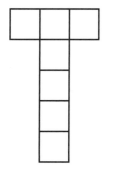

5.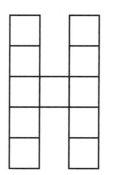

6.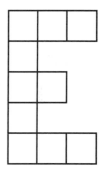

_____   _____   _____

7.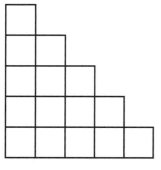

8.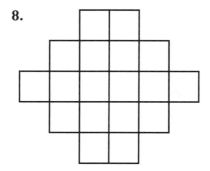

9.

_____   _____   _____

Reteach **RW135**

Name _____

LESSON 26.4

Area of Solid Figures

You can find the total area that covers a solid figure by finding the area of each face.

A Cube

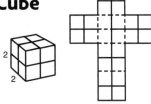

Each face has an area of 2 × 2, or 4 square units. There are 6 faces.
The total area is 4 + 4 + 4 + 4 + 4 + 4 = 24 or 6 × 4 = 24 square units.

A Rectangular Solid

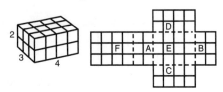

Area of face A: 3 × 2 = 6
Area of face B: 3 × 2 = 6
Area of face C: 2 × 4 = 8
Area of face D: 2 × 4 = 8
Area of face E: 3 × 4 = 12
Area of face F: 3 × 4 = 12
Add the 6 areas: 6 + 6 + 8 + 8 + 12 + 12 = 52 square units

Find the total area that covers each solid figure.

1.

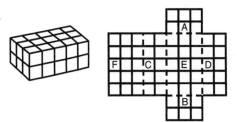

2.

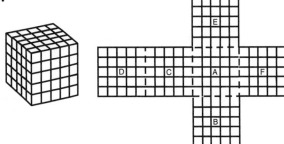

Area of face A: _____

Area of face B: _____

Area of face C: _____

Area of each side: _____

Area of face D: _____

Total Area: _____

Area of face E: _____

Area of face F: _____

Total Area: _____

RW136 Reteach

Name _____

LESSON 26.5

Problem Solving Skill

Make Generalizations

Matthew has 12 yards of fencing. He wants to make a pen for his rabbits. Which pen has the greatest area?

      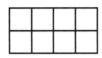   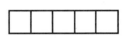

perimeter = 12 yd   perimeter = 12 yd   perimeter = 12 yd
area = 9 sq yd   area = 8 sq yd   area = 5 sq yd

The pen with the largest area is a square with 3 yards on each side.

Find the perimeter and area of each figure.

1. perimeter = _____ units

   area = _____ sq units

2. perimeter = _____ units

   area = _____ sq units

3. perimeter = _____ units

   area = _____ sq units

4. perimeter = _____ units

   area = _____ sq units

5. Draw 3 different rectangles that each has a perimeter of 14 units. Circle the rectangle with the greatest area.

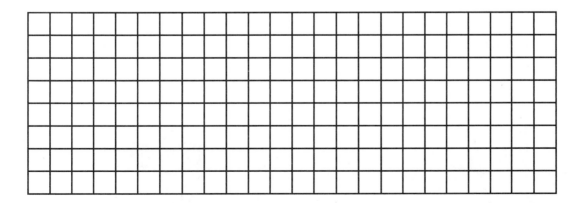

Reteach RW137

Name _____

Estimate and Find Volume

When you measure **volume**, you measure the amount of space a solid figure takes up.

To measure the volume of a solid, find the number of **cubic units** needed to fill the solid.

1 cubic unit

Here are two ways to find the volume of a rectangular solid.

You can count

There are 2 rows of 5 cubes (10 cubes) in each layer of this solid.

There are 3 layers.

So, 10 + 10 + 10 = 30 cubic units.

You can multiply

3 layers × 10 cubes per layer = 30 cubic units. .

So, the volume of the cube is 30 cubic units..

Find the volume of each solid. Write the volume in cubic units.

1.

   There are _____ rows of _____ cubes or _____ on the bottom of this solid.

   There are _____ layers with 14 cubes in them. So, 14 + 14 + 14 = _____

2.

   Length × Width × Height = Volume

   _____ × _____ × _____
   ↓
   _____ × _____ = _____

   _____

3.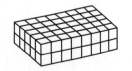

   Total Area: _____

4.

   Total Area: _____

RW138 Reteach

Name _____ LESSON 27.1

Count Parts of a Whole

A **fraction** is a number that names a part of a whole or set. The **numerator** tells how many parts are being counted. The **denominator** tells how many equal parts are in the whole.

$\dfrac{2}{3}$ ← numerator
← denominator

A fraction tells about itself. For example, $\frac{3}{4}$ tells you that a whole is divided into 4 equal parts and that 3 of those parts are being counted. So, you can draw and shade it:

 or or or

---

1.   Number of shaded parts: _____

    Number of equal parts: _____

    Fraction for the shaded part of the circle: _____

2.   Number of shaded parts: _____

    Number of equal parts: _____

    Fraction for the shaded part of the square: _____

3.   Number of shaded parts: _____

    Number of equal parts: _____

    Fraction for the shaded part of the rectangle: _____

4. Brian had a piece of rope. He cut it into 8 equal parts. He used 3 of the parts on a project. What fraction of the rope did Brian use?

    a. How many parts did Brian use? _____

    b. How many equal parts make up the rope? _____

    c. What fraction of the rope did he use? _____

Name _____

LESSON 27.2

Count Parts of a Group

You can use fractions to name part of a group.

   numerator ⟶ $\boxed{3}$ number of shaded blocks
denominator ⟶ $\boxed{4}$ total number of blocks

Write the fraction that names the part of the group that is shaded.

1.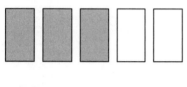

2.

3.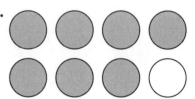

4.

5.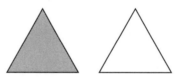

6.

7.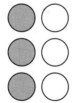

8.

9.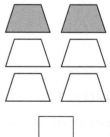

RW140 Reteach

Name _____

LESSON 27.3

Equivalent Fractions

Equivalent fractions are two or more fractions that name the same amount.

The following will help you make a model of some equivalent fractions.

- Cut 4 pieces of string that are each 8 inches long.
- Tape one string lengthwise on a piece of paper. This will be your model for one whole, or 1.
- Cut the second string in half. Tape the 2 pieces end-to-end next to the first string. Each piece will be your model for $\frac{1}{2}$.

Notice that 2 halves or $\frac{2}{2} = 1$.

- Cut the third string into 4 equal parts. Tape the 4 pieces end-to-end next to the second string. Each piece will be your model for $\frac{1}{4}$.

Notice that 4 fourths or $\frac{4}{4} = \frac{2}{2} = 1$.

- Cut the fourth string into 8 equal parts. Tape the 8 pieces end-to-end next to the third string. Each piece will be your model for $\frac{1}{8}$.

Notice that 8 eighths or $\frac{8}{8} = \frac{4}{4} = \frac{2}{2} = 1$.

These are equivalent fractions: $\frac{8}{8} = \frac{4}{4} = \frac{2}{2}$.

Find an equivalent fraction for each. Use your string model.

1. $\frac{1}{4} = \frac{\Box}{8}$
2. $\frac{2}{2} = \frac{\Box}{8}$
3. $\frac{3}{4} = \frac{\Box}{8}$

4. $\frac{1}{2} = \frac{\Box}{4}$
5. $1 = \frac{\Box}{8}$
6. $\frac{2}{4} = \frac{\Box}{8}$

7. $\frac{1}{2} = \frac{\Box}{8}$
8. $\frac{2}{2} = \frac{\Box}{4}$
9. $\frac{4}{4} = \frac{\Box}{8}$

Reteach **RW141**

Name _____

LESSON 27.4

Compare and Order Fractions

Fraction bars can help you compare fractions.
Example: Compare $\frac{1}{3}$ and $\frac{1}{2}$.

The bar for $\frac{1}{2}$ is longer than the bar for $\frac{1}{3}$. So, $\frac{1}{3} < \frac{1}{2}$ or $\frac{1}{2} > \frac{1}{3}$.

Tiles can help you compare parts of groups.
Example: Compare $\frac{2}{5}$ and $\frac{4}{5}$.

4 tiles are more than 2 tiles.

So, $\frac{2}{5} < \frac{4}{5}$ or $\frac{4}{5} > \frac{2}{5}$.

Compare. Write <, >, or = for each ○.

1.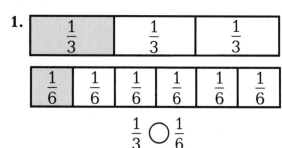

   $\frac{1}{3}$ ○ $\frac{1}{6}$

2.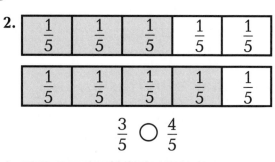

   $\frac{3}{5}$ ○ $\frac{4}{5}$

3.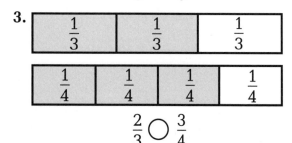

   $\frac{2}{3}$ ○ $\frac{3}{4}$

4.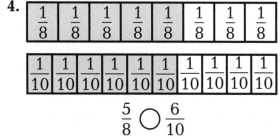

   $\frac{5}{8}$ ○ $\frac{6}{10}$

5. Order $\frac{1}{3}$, $\frac{1}{2}$, and $\frac{1}{4}$ from greatest to least.

   _____

RW142 Reteach

Name _____

LESSON 27.5

Problem Solving Strategy
Make a Model

At track practice, 3 team members each ran a fraction of a mile. Tiko ran $\frac{3}{8}$ mile. Raoul ran $\frac{2}{3}$ mile. Lin ran $\frac{3}{6}$ mile. Who ran the farthest?

1. What are you asked to find? _____

2. How will you do this? _____

3. What information will you use? _____

_____

You can make a model of the problem using fraction bars. Line up fraction bars for $\frac{3}{8}$, $\frac{2}{3}$, and $\frac{3}{6}$. Compare the lengths of the fraction bars. Now you can compare distances.

4. Who ran the farthest? _____

---

5. At the next track practice, Tiko ran $\frac{3}{4}$ mile, Raoul ran $\frac{4}{6}$ mile, and Lin ran $\frac{7}{8}$ mile. Use shading on the bars below to show how far each team member ran. Then answer the question.

Tiko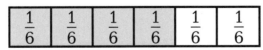

Raoul

Lin

Who ran the farthest? _____

Reteach RW143

Name _____

LESSON 28.1

Add Fractions

Fractions that have the same denominator are called **like fractions**.

Remember:
$\frac{1}{2}$ → numerator
→ denominator

You can add like fractions by counting fraction bars.

$\frac{2}{6} + \frac{3}{6} = \blacksquare$

$\frac{2}{6}$ + $\frac{3}{6}$ → $\frac{1}{6}, \frac{2}{6}, \frac{3}{6}, \frac{4}{6}, \frac{5}{6}$

So, $\frac{2}{6} + \frac{3}{6} = \frac{5}{6}$.

Find the sum.

1. $\frac{1}{3} + \frac{1}{3} =$ _____

2. $\frac{3}{8} + \frac{4}{8} =$ _____

Find each sum. You may wish to use fraction bars.

3. $\frac{3}{9} + \frac{4}{9} =$ _____

4. $\frac{1}{10} + \frac{5}{10} =$ _____

5. $\frac{2}{5} + \frac{1}{5} =$ _____

6. $\frac{1}{4} + \frac{2}{4} =$ _____

7. $\frac{2}{9} + \frac{6}{9} =$ _____

8. $\frac{6}{12} + \frac{4}{12} =$ _____

9. $\frac{4}{8} + \frac{2}{8} =$ _____

10. $\frac{1}{8} + \frac{5}{8} =$ _____

11. $\frac{1}{2} + \frac{1}{2} =$ _____

12. $\frac{1}{6} + \frac{2}{6} =$ _____

13. $\frac{2}{8} + \frac{2}{8} =$ _____

14. $\frac{4}{10} + \frac{5}{10} =$ _____

RW144   Reteach

Name _____

LESSON 28.2

Add Fractions

You can use fraction bars to add fractions and to find their **simplest form**. A fraction is in simplest form when it uses the largest fraction bar possible.

$\frac{2}{6} + \frac{2}{6} = \blacksquare$

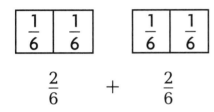

Step 1

$\frac{2}{6} + \frac{2}{6}$

So, $\frac{2}{6} + \frac{2}{6} = \frac{4}{6}$.

Step 2

Find the largest fraction bar or bars that are the same length.

So, $\frac{4}{6}$ in simplest form is $\frac{2}{3}$.

Find the sum. Write the answer in simplest form.

1. $\frac{1}{6} + \frac{2}{6} = $ _____

2. $\frac{2}{10} + \frac{4}{10} = $ _____

Find the sum. Write the answer in simplest form. Use fraction bars if you wish.

3. $\frac{1}{9} + \frac{2}{9} = $ _____

4. $\frac{1}{10} + \frac{5}{10} = $ _____

5. $\frac{2}{4} + \frac{2}{4} = $ _____

6. $\frac{1}{8} + \frac{3}{8} = $ _____

7. $\frac{2}{12} + \frac{2}{12} = $ _____

8. $\frac{3}{12} + \frac{6}{12} = $ _____

9. $\frac{4}{10} + \frac{1}{10} = $ _____

10. $\frac{1}{8} + \frac{5}{8} = $ _____

11. $\frac{1}{2} + \frac{1}{2} = $ _____

Reteach **RW145**

Name _____

LESSON 28.3

Subtract Fractions

Fractions that have the same denominator are called **like fractions**.

You can subtract like fractions by taking away fraction bars.

Remember:
$\dfrac{1}{2}$ → numerator
→ denominator

$\dfrac{3}{6} - \dfrac{2}{6} = \blacksquare$

Example

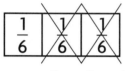

So, $\dfrac{3}{6} - \dfrac{2}{6} = \dfrac{1}{6}$.

Compare. Find the difference.

1. | $\dfrac{1}{5}$ | $\dfrac{1}{5}$ | $\dfrac{1}{5}$ | $\dfrac{1}{5}$ |

   $\dfrac{4}{5} - \dfrac{3}{5} =$ _____

2. | $\dfrac{1}{4}$ | $\dfrac{1}{4}$ | $\dfrac{1}{4}$ |

   $\dfrac{3}{4} - \dfrac{2}{4} =$ _____

Find each difference. Use fraction bars.

3. $\dfrac{7}{8} - \dfrac{2}{8} =$ _____

4. $\dfrac{5}{10} - \dfrac{1}{10} =$ _____

5. $\dfrac{2}{5} - \dfrac{1}{5} =$ _____

6. $\dfrac{4}{4} - \dfrac{2}{4} =$ _____

7. $\dfrac{2}{3} - \dfrac{1}{3} =$ _____

8. $\dfrac{6}{12} - \dfrac{4}{12} =$ _____

9. $\dfrac{5}{6} - \dfrac{2}{6} =$ _____

10. $\dfrac{6}{8} - \dfrac{3}{8} =$ _____

11. $\dfrac{8}{12} - \dfrac{3}{12} =$ _____

12. $\dfrac{4}{5} - \dfrac{2}{5} =$ _____

13. $\dfrac{8}{10} - \dfrac{3}{10} =$ _____

14. $\dfrac{5}{8} - \dfrac{1}{8} =$ _____

Name _____

LESSON 28.4

Subtract Fractions

You can use fraction bars to subtract fractions and to find their simplest form. A fraction is in simplest form when it uses the largest fraction bar or bars possible.

$\frac{5}{6} - \frac{2}{6} = \blacksquare$

Step 1

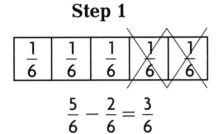

$\frac{5}{6} - \frac{2}{6} = \frac{3}{6}$

Step 2

Find the largest fraction bar that is the same length.

$\frac{3}{6} = \frac{1}{2}$

Compare. Find the difference. Write the answer in simplest form.

1.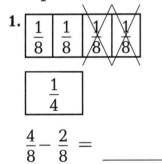

   $\frac{4}{8} - \frac{2}{8} = $ _____

2.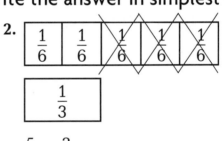

   $\frac{5}{6} - \frac{3}{6} = $ _____

Find each difference. Write the answer in simplest form. Use fraction bars.

3. $\frac{3}{4} - \frac{1}{4} = $ _____

4. $\frac{9}{10} - \frac{4}{10} = $ _____

5. $\frac{8}{10} - \frac{4}{10} = $ _____

6. $\frac{3}{4} - \frac{2}{4} = $ _____

7. $\frac{6}{12} - \frac{2}{12} = $ _____

8. $\frac{11}{12} - \frac{3}{12} = $ _____

9. $\frac{7}{10} - \frac{2}{10} = $ _____

10. $\frac{8}{8} - \frac{2}{8} = $ _____

11. $\frac{9}{12} - \frac{3}{12} = $ _____

Reteach RW147

Problem Solving Skill

Reasonable Answers

When you solve a problem, always check that your answer is reasonable and makes sense.

Read the following problem.

Nick mailed a box that weighed 1 pound. The box contained 3 books. One book weighed $\frac{3}{8}$ pound. A second book weighed $\frac{2}{8}$ pound. How much did the third book weigh?

1. How much did the first two books weigh together?

   _____

2. Using eighths, how can you write 1 pound as a fraction?

   _____

3. How much did the third book weigh?

   _____

4. How do you know your answer is reasonable?

   _____

   _____

5. Fred planted $\frac{3}{6}$ of his flower garden before lunch and $\frac{2}{6}$ after lunch. He plans to plant the rest tomorrow. How much of the garden will he plant tomorrow?

6. Jane walked $\frac{2}{8}$ of a mile to school and then $\frac{2}{8}$ of a mile to the store. She walked the rest of the mile to her friend's house. How much of the mile did she walk to her friend's house?

Name _____

LESSON 29.1

Relate Fractions and Decimals

You can write a fraction or a decimal to tell what part is shaded.

Model	Fraction	Decimal	Read
	$\frac{4}{10}$	0.4	four tenths
	$\frac{3}{10}$	0.3	three tenths

Complete the table.

	Model	Fraction	Decimal	Read
1.		$\frac{\Box}{\Box}$		
2.				
3.				
4.				
5.				

Reteach RW149

Tenths

Decimals can show **tenths**.

Three out of 10 equal parts are shaded. Three tenths are shaded.

Three tenths can be written as a fraction: $\frac{3}{10}$.

Three tenths can also be written as a decimal: 0.3.

Write a fraction and a decimal to show how many equal parts are shaded.

	Fraction	Decimal

1.   _____   _____

2.   _____   _____

3.   _____   _____

4.   _____   _____

Name _____

LESSON 29.3

Hundredths

A whole can be divided into 100 equal parts called **hundredths.**

Six parts out of 100 equal parts are shaded. Six hundredths are shaded.

Write as a fraction: $\frac{6}{100}$.

Write as a decimal: 0.06.

Twenty-six parts out of 100 equal parts are shaded. Twenty-six hundredths are shaded.

Write as a fraction: $\frac{26}{100}$.

Write as a decimal: 0.26.

Write a fraction and a decimal to show what part of each decimal model is shaded.

1. Fraction: _____

   Decimal: _____

2. Fraction: _____

   Decimal: _____

3. Fraction: _____

   Decimal: _____

4. Fraction: _____

   Decimal: _____

5. 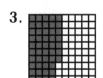 Fraction: _____

   Decimal: _____

6. Fraction: _____

   Decimal: _____

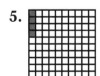

Reteach RW151

Name _____

LESSON 29.4

Read and Write Decimals

You can use a place-value chart to help you write a decimal in 3 different ways.

Ones	Tenths	Hundredths
0 .	5	3

Standard Form: 0.53
Word Form: fifty-three hundredths
Expanded form: 0.5 + 0.03

Write the word form and expanded form for each decimal.

1.
Ones	Tenths	Hundredths
0 .	3	1

word form: _____

expanded form: _____

2.
Ones	Tenths	Hundredths
0 .	2	8

word form: _____

expanded form: _____

3.
Ones	Tenths	Hundredths
0 .	5	9

word form: _____

expanded form: _____

4.
Ones	Tenths	Hundredths
0 .	5	5

word form: _____

expanded form: _____

Write *tenths* or *hundredths*.

5. 0.65 = 6 tenths

   5 _____

6. 0.94 = 9 _____

   4 hundredths

7. 0.09 = 0 _____

   9 hundredths

8. 0.47 = 4 tenths

   7 _____

Write the missing number.

9. 0.92 = ____ tenths

   2 hundredths

10. 0.36 = ____ tenths

    6 hundredths

RW152 Reteach

Name _____

LESSON 29.5

Compare and Order Decimals

You can compare decimals using a place-value chart or decimal models.

Compare 1.32 and 1.18.

Ones	Tenths	Hundredths
1	3	2
1	1	8

↑ 3 > 1

Start at the greatest place value and compare the digits in each place.
Since 3 > 1, 1.32 > 1.18.

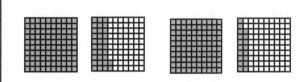

1.32 > 1.18

Another way to compare decimals is to use a number line.

Locate each decimal on the number line. The decimal farther to the right is greater.   1.32 > 1.18

Compare. Write < or > for each ○.

1.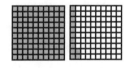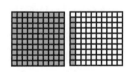

   1.12 ○ 1.09

2.

   0.65 ○ 1.13

3.
Ones	Tenths	Hundredths
5	0	8
5	6	1

   5.08 ○ 5.61

4.
Ones	Tenths	Hundredths
3	2	8
1	9	9

   3.28 ○ 1.99

Use the number line to order the decimals from least to greatest.

5. 0.3, 0.8, 0.6

6. 1.0, 0.6, 0.1

_____   _____

Reteach **RW153**

Problem Solving Skill
Reasonable Answers

When you solve a problem, always check that your answer is reasonable and makes sense.

Read the following problem.

Mickey runs 3.6 miles each day to get ready for a marathon. He only ran part of this distance when he got a side ache. When he stopped, he said he had at least 4 more miles to run. Is his estimate reasonable?

1. Solve the problem.

   Which is greater, 3.6 miles or 4 miles? _____

   Is it possible that Mickey still has 4 miles to run? Explain.

   _____

   _____

   What would be a reasonable estimate of how much farther Mickey has to run? _____

2. Ginger runs 2.5 miles each day. Today she ran more than this. Is it reasonable to say she ran 1.8 miles today? Explain why or why not.

3. Kevin bought 2 apples. They each weighed 0.4 of a pound. The checkout clerk charged him for a total of 0.8 pounds. Is that total reasonable? Explain why or why not. _____

4. James spent $8.23 on dinner. He paid with a $10 bill. Is it reasonable to say James got $3.00 back in change? Explain why or why not. _____

5. Lucy spent $4.25 for lunch. She got $0.75 in change. Is it reasonable to say she gave the clerk a $5-bill? Explain.

Reteach

Name _____

LESSON 30.1

Relate Fractions and Money

Mr. Loo was asked to donate money to a charity. He was told that $\frac{1}{4}$ of every dollar donated would be given to a food pantry in his town. How much money from every dollar is donated to the food pantry?

4 quarters = 1 dollar = $1.00

$0.25 $0.25 $0.25 $0.25

$\frac{1}{4}$ of a dollar = $0.25

So, $0.25 out of every dollar goes to the food pantry.

Write the amount of money shown. Then write the amount as a fraction of a dollar.

1.

_____

2.

_____

3.

_____

4.

_____

5.

_____

6.

_____

7.

_____

8.

_____

Reteach   RW155

Name _____

LESSON 30.2

Relate Decimals and Money

You can think about dimes as tenths and pennies as hundredths.

 =     =

100 pennies = 1 dollar
A penny is $\frac{1}{100}$ or 0.01 of a dollar.

10 dimes = 1 dollar
A dime is $\frac{1}{10}$ or 0.10 of a dollar.

$0.57

Ones	Tenths	Hundredths
0 .	5	7

0.57 = 57 hundredths

0.57 = 5 tenths 7 hundredths

$0.57

Dollars	Dimes	Pennies
0 .	5	7

$0.57 = 57 pennies = 57 hundredths of a dollar

$0.57 = 5 dimes 7 pennies = 5 tenths 7 hundredths of a dollar

---

Write the money amount for each fraction of a dollar.

1. $\frac{30}{100}$ 2. $\frac{75}{100}$ 3. $\frac{18}{100}$ 4. $\frac{45}{100}$

   _____   _____   _____   _____

Write the money amount for each.

5. 7 hundredths of a dollar

6. 29 hundredths of a dollar

7. 16 hundredths of a dollar

   _____   _____   _____

Write the missing numbers. Use the fewest coins possible.

8. $0.98 = ___ dimes ___ pennies   9. $0.52 = ___ dimes ___ pennies

10. $0.37 = ___ dimes ___ pennies   11. $0.13 = ___ dimes ___ pennies

RW156   Reteach

Name _____

LESSON 30.3

Add and Subtract Decimals and Money

You can use decimal models to add and subtract decimals and money.

0.20 + 0.25 = 0.45   0.45 − 0.20 = 0.25

You can also use pencil and paper to add and subtract decimals and money.

Step 1: Line up the decimal points.

Step 2: Add or subtract as you would with whole numbers.

Step 3: Write the decimal point in the answer.

```
        1                5 15
      0.28             $ 0.6̶5̶
    + 0.15            −$ 0.18
    ──────            ───────
      0 43              $0 47         0.43    $0.47
```

Add or subtract.

1.
0.45
+ 0.13
─────

2.
0.69
− 0.53
─────

3.
0.50
− 0.17
─────

4.
0.37
+ 0.26
─────

5. 0.33
  + 0.24
  ─────

6. 0.80
  − 0.55
  ─────

7. 0.18
  + 0.19
  ─────

8. $ 0.94
  −$ 0.62
  ──────

9. $ 0.68
  −$ 0.49
  ──────

10. 0.29
   + 0.37
   ─────

11. 0.75
   − 0.49
   ─────

12. $ 0.44
   +$ 0.25
   ──────

Reteach RW157

Name _____

LESSON 30.4

Problem Solving Strategy
Break Problems into Simpler Parts

When you solve a problem, sometimes it is helpful to break the problem into simpler parts.

Read the following problem.

Lance has $5 to buy toys. If he buys 1 yo-yo and 2 bags of marbles, how much money will he have left?

Item	Price
yo-yo	$1.39
marbles	$0.52 per bag
kite	$1.09
whistle	$0.89

1. Underline what you are asked to find.

2. What information will you use? _____
   _____

3. Is there information you will not use? If so what?
   _____

4. What strategy can you use to solve the problem?
   _____

5. How can you use the strategy to solve the problem?
   _____
   _____

   Solve the problem.

6. _____

Use the table of prices above. Break the problems into simpler parts to solve.

7. Julia has $3. She bought 4 bags of marbles. How much change should she receive?

8. Robert has $4. He bought a whistle, a kite, and a yo-yo. How much change did he receive?

RW158 Reteach